Managing the Interactive Classroom

A Collection of Articles

Edited by Kay Burke

SkyLight
Professional
Development

Arlington Heights, Illinois

Managing the Interactive Classroom

A Collection of Articles

The title of this book, *Managing the Interactive Classroom,* may seem like a paradox to some people. Managing sounds controlling—if you manage your money, you account for it by watching carefully what you spend and what you save. If you manage a company, you are responsible for monitoring and controlling what everyone does. Managing a classroom, too, brings to mind the traditional image of a teacher in firm control of the students. The teacher is standing in front of the classroom, book in hand, while the students sit in rows and read and write quietly. The students have trays to place their papers in; the homework assignment is posted on the board; and students know to raise their hands and to line up for recess. The traditional teacher-manager organizes the classroom for maximum efficiency and production, not too much differently than the plant manager or store manager.

Today's modern teacher-manager uses some of the same organizational strategies as the traditional teacher-manager. He or she still sets high expectations and organizes the classroom for maximum efficiency, but for the most part, students are not sitting in rows listening to the teacher lecture.

The Philosophy of Cooperative Classroom Management

All our lives, we search for ways to satisfy our needs for love, belonging, caring, sharing, and cooperation. If a student feels no sense of belonging in school, no sense of being involved in caring and concern, that child will pay little attention to academic subjects.—William Glasser

Contrary to the stimulus/response psychology that has been used in education to try to make students learn and behave, William Glasser and Alfie Kohn both advocate including students in the decision-making process in the classroom. Students who take an active role in setting the climate for their learning and who understand the reasons why they should treat others with respect exhibit prosocial behaviors because they want to—not because they have to.

Glasser says that coercion has never had a long-term effect on curbing negative behaviors. In addition, Kohn feels that we tend to focus too much on "curbing" negative behaviors rather than "promoting" positive ones.

Teachers can set the climate for a sharing, cooperative classroom by modeling prosocial behaviors and by helping students act responsibly. In addition, teachers in restructured schools should be less concerned with maintaining control and more concerned with empowering students to take responsibility for their own behavior. Kohn says that even the word "discipline"

Glasser: I think that the commission missed the problem. The problem is that at least half of all students are making little or no effort to learn, because they don't believe that school satisfies their needs. To make school harder—to increase the length of the school year or the school day, to assign more homework, to require more courses in science and mathematics—is not going to reach those students. It's only going to increase the separation between the half who are already working and the half who are not.

> The problem is that at least half of all students are making little or no effort to learn, because they don't believe that school satisfies their needs.

The commission tried to solve the problem traditionally, by stimulating teachers and students in the hope that they would work harder—regardless of whether what is being asked of them is satisfying or not. Stimulus/response psychology has never worked in the past, and it won't work now. We can't do anything *to* people, or really even *for* people, to get them to produce more. We have to change the school itself, so that students look at it and say, "In this school and with these teachers I can satisfy my needs, if I work hard." The commission did not address itself to this basic psychological issue, and thus its report will have no impact on the huge numbers of students who refuse to work hard in schools that do not satisfy their needs.

Kappan: In your new book, Control Theory in the Classroom, *you have suggested specific means by which secondary schools can deal more effectively with unmotivated students. Before we examine the changes you propose, would you explain the theory undergirding those changes?*

Glasser: Nothing will change for the better until educators and others understand that stimulus/response theory—under which everyone (including the commission) currently operates—is wrong. According to stimulus/response theory, human behavior is caused by external events. For example, a person stops at a traffic light because it turns red.

By contrast, the major premise of control theory is that all human behavior is generated by what goes on *inside* the behaving person. Therefore, a person stops at a traffic light *not* because the light turns red, but because that person says, "I want to stay alive." In other words, all that we get from the outside world is information. We then choose to act on that information in the way we believe is best for us.

Kappan: Could you give us an example in a school setting?

Glasser: What students get from school—from their English class, for example—is information. They then ask, "Will this information satisfy my needs, and should I work hard to get more of it?" As a society, we're failing to understand that students will not work in classes that do not satisfy their needs. It doesn't help to say to these students, "You should appreciate the fact that what we do is for your benefit. Look at how many students are working. You should work hard, too."

It's not that students aren't working in schools; as many as half *do* work in good schools, because they see schoolwork as satisfying. My point is, if half of all students are *not* working because they perceive that school will not satisfy their needs, we have to attend to the fact that a major institution in our society—perhaps the one on which we spend the most money—follows a theory that does not address itself to the needs of more than half of its clients. The old theory, "We can make 'em work; all we have to do is get tough," has never produced intellectual effort in the history of the world, and it certainly won't work in this situation.

Kappan: What are the needs of students that the schools are failing to address?

Glasser: The needs of students are the same as those of everyone else. As I mentioned with regard to the traffic light, we all need to survive. But survival is not the major concern of most American students. They believe that they are going to survive, and they don't see school as related to that survival—even

> The old theory, "We can make 'em work; all we have to do is get tough," has never produced intellectual effort in the history of the world.

structure. From birth we *must* struggle—we have no choice—to try to survive and to try to find some love, some power, some fun, and some freedom. To the extent that we can satisfy these needs on a regular basis, we gain effective control of our lives.

Kappan: How does control theory deal with the problem of discipline in the schools?

Glasser: Understanding control theory is crucial both to understanding and to solving the problem of discipline in the schools. There are a plethora of discipline programs on the market these days, but all of them are based on stimulus/response psychology—on doing something *to* the student (a scare technique, a small punishment, writing the student's name on the chalkboard, or some other consequence). For students who want to behave, these small stimuli serve as reminders that they are out of order, but for students whose needs are not being satisfied, they are useless. Our jails are filled with people who have been disciplined up to their ears—and, because most of them are lonely and powerless, they continue to commit crimes.

> Understanding control theory is crucial both to understanding and to solving the problem of discipline in the schools.

According to control theory, discipline problems do not occur in classrooms in which students' needs are satisfied. An administrator who is concerned about the discipline problems in his or her school has only to mentally review the behaviors of the teaching staff to discover that six or seven teachers *never* complain of discipline problems. And the administrator has only to observe in the classrooms of those six or seven teachers to discover that they run their classes according to the concepts of control theory. Their students not only like them but also have a sense of importance, because they take part in class meetings and discussions that allow them to feel accepted and significant in the *academic* environment. Since discipline problems do not exist in the classrooms of such teachers, good discipline is clearly a matter of running the schools so that students say, "This school makes sense to me. I won't break the rules of a place in which I can get what I need."

Take a close look at any school function where the students are in good order, and you'll find satisfied students. Does the band teacher, the chorus teacher, the drama teacher, or the football coach have problems with students not working, not paying attention, not behaving? Rarely. That's because, in these situations (and you'll notice that I've picked out, for the most part, group situations), the students are satisfied.

Kappan: Would you describe the restructured secondary school, as you envision it?

Glasser: In the beginning, the teachers, the administrators, the school board, and as many parents as can be lured to the school would be enrolled in a course or a series of discussion groups led by someone who understands control theory. This would help them begin to understand the difference between control theory (which says that motivation comes from within and that we all have to figure out satisfying ways to live our lives) and stimulus/response theory (which got schools into all this difficulty in the first place). It would also help the participants begin to use control theory in their own lives. This is the key to restructuring the schools.

Kappan: That all sounds very theoretical.

Glasser: I know it does, but it's really not. If we attempt to put together a control-theory school in which people neither understand nor believe in control theory, it just won't happen. So widespread understanding and use of the theory is the first step. I'm working on some films and other materials, which I hope will be ready by next year, to help schools get started.

Kappan: And the next step?

Glasser: The next step is to ask ourselves, "Where in schools do things work well now?" I've already mentioned some of those areas: the band and the orchestra, the drama program, athletics, the school newspaper and the yearbook. In each of these situations, students are working together in some sort of a group that I prefer to call a learning team, though this kind of enlives: transferring from the elementary school to the junior high) to tell me how many students are working in school. Youngsters attending an inner-city school in Detroit told me that 25% of their peers are working and 75% are not. Students living in affluent locales tend to say that 50% of their peers are working in school, but the figure never goes higher than that.

Then I've asked these youngsters, "Did some students who aren't working now work in elementary school?" And they've responded, "Yes, they did. Sometimes in fourth, fifth, and even sixth grade they were working." So I've prodded, "Then why aren't they working now?" And the youngsters have told me, "Well, it all changed when we went to junior high. The teachers in junior high have less time for students; their attitude is, 'Do it, and don't ask questions.'" These youngsters are really saying that junior high school is much less satisfying than elementary school, because in the junior high they feel so unimportant.

> If I say to the secondary people, "The fault's in the elementary schools," then the secondary schools will never change.

The ideas I present in *Control Theory in the Classroom* are not exclusively for secondary school; elementary schools could certainly profit from them, as well. But I really believe that the secondary schools will never improve their performance unless they put these ideas to use. Following stimulus/response theory is like using a manual typewriter: no matter what you do or how hard you hit it, you can only do so much. And that's where our secondary schools are today. No matter how many external stimuli we apply, the situation will not change. If we could begin to restructure secondary schools in the ways I've suggested, elementary educators would see the advantages of bringing these ideas into their classrooms, and change would follow in the elementary schools, as well.

But if I say to the secondary people, "The fault's in the elementary schools," then the secondary schools will never change, because secondary educators believe that the students sent to them are ill-prepared. For this reason, I think we have to focus particularly on the junior high school or middle school, and then move these ideas up as well as down.

Kappan: In your book, you draw a parallel between athletic teams and learning teams, and you've alluded to the similarity between the two here. Would you explain in greater detail . . . just why the two kinds of teams are similar?

Glasser: They're very similar; in both instances, progress depends on what the team members do together. One basketball player may average 30 points per game and another player may average only two points per game, but the first player is not necessarily considered better than the second. The player who scores only two points may feed the ball to the player who scores 30 points; without his or her accurate passes, the high scorer would be helpless. The coach doesn't give the high scorer a better grade than the low scorer. Since the team's grade is the final score, which members of the team earn together, the coach tries to teach them to cooperate, to talk to each other on the floor, to pass the ball off, to make each game as much a team effort as possible.

Most classrooms today are exactly the opposite, but they don't have to be. There's tradition, but there's no law saying that students must work alone, never sharing what they do.

Kappan: Could you be more specific about ways to use this team approach in the classroom?

Glasser: Why shouldn't students put their heads together and produce a team effort in mathematics, in history, in English? They could write a skit together, discuss a book together, write a paper together, do some research together. That's the way they're going to work in the world outside of school. The pattern for team effort is already in place in band and orchestra, on the school newspaper, and in athletics. The only place that teams are missing is in the classroom.

Recently, as I mention in my book, I visited a class that was ending its first learning-team assignment with some skits. When I arrived, the teacher told me that one of his good students would probably not be present for the activity. When I asked why not, he told me that she was a member of the soccer team and had been excused from her last period class to go to a game.

But when the students came in, she was there—and she played a major role in one of the skits.

She had to dash off after class, but the next day her teacher asked her, "Why didn't you go to the soccer game instead of coming to English class?" She responded that her team had worked hard in preparing its skit, and she didn't want to let the other members of the group down. So she'd arranged to get to the game by herself, instead of leaving early with the team.

If she had been working alone, she wouldn't have given a thought to being late for the game just to work by herself in class. She stayed because she was a member of the team. Clearly, when learning teams work well, comparing them to athletic teams is apt.

> **Only individuals who are very exceptional can obtain a sense of power by themselves. The rest of us have to obtain a sense of power through membership in some sort of team.**

Kappan: Can you offer any advice to teachers on setting up learning teams?

Glasser: As a general rule, teachers should *select* the members of learning teams. A four-member team, for example, might include one top-notch student, one low-achieving student, and a couple of average students. But teachers will find that youngsters work harder on teams, and teachers won't always be able to tell which team member was formerly the poor student and which team member was formerly the good student. When the so-called poor student says, "I feel important here; they depend on me; they encourage me; they want me to produce—and I'm *going* to produce, because I don't want to let anyone down," he or she is no longer a poor student.

As I said earlier, only individuals who are very exceptional can obtain a sense of power by themselves. The rest of us have to obtain a sense of power through membership in some sort of team: a family, a group at work, an athletic team, whatever. Note that the Nobel Prize is as often given to a group of people who worked together on a project as to an individual. The people who win Nobel Prizes are stars—but even they work together.

Kappan: How will school people have to change, in order to use learning teams effectively?

Glasser: Teachers will have to change the way they look at themselves. And to make that possible, administrators will have to change the way they look at teachers.

Too often, today's administrators view teachers as workers who can be stimulated into greater productivity. In schools that operate under the stimulus/response theory, teachers are expected to do what they're told and produce educated students. This view of teachers as workers permeates our whole society.

But a student is not an inert object to be worked on; a student is a human being with needs. And school systems must recognize that everyone will benefit, if the schools satisfy students' needs in ways that encourage students to learn those things that society considers essential. Teachers who simply say to their students, "This is the essential knowledge; learn it," are not effective. That approach works only with those students who agree with this point of view—up to 50% in the best schools and a lot less in most schools.

> A student is not an inert object to be worked on; a student is a human being with needs.

Kappan: Then what is the teacher's role?

Glasser: The teacher's job is to facilitate. I don't like to use the word *motivate,* because it's an "external" word. Like the rest of us, students have plenty of motivation. The question is, Will they be motivated to learn what we believe they should learn? We can't force "our" knowledge down students' throats—though that's what the public is asking teachers to do, in a sense, when it tells teachers to raise Scholastic Aptitude Test scores. *Teachers* can't raise SAT scores. Teachers can only teach in a way that makes students *want* to learn. When students learn, they do well on the SAT.

The teacher's role is to set up a workplace that persuades students to say, "Aha! I see that, if I work in this place, it's going to satisfy me. I see, in this place, that knowledge is power."

Teachers can't *make* students learn, but they can certainly set things up so that students *want* to learn.

As I note in my book, you can lead a horse to water, but you can't make him drink. However, Madeline Hunter (a good friend of mine and an outstanding educator) points out that you can't make him drink, but you *can* put some salt in his oats. And she's 100% correct. The teacher who's a good manager will figure out how to put some salt in the oats. That's what *Control Theory in the Classroom* is all about.

> Teachers can't *make* students learn, but they can certainly set things up so that students *want* to learn.

Kappan: In addition to changing their role rather radically, in the ways that you've just described, what other problems will teachers face as they try to implement learning teams? And how can they cope with those problems?

Glasser: The first thing that teachers will be concerned about is losing power, losing control. They'll ask themselves, "Can I trust students to work together? Will the good students do all the work, while the poor students just hitchhike along? Will students go home and complain, 'Oh, the teacher is making me work in a group, and it's slowing me down'? If they do, how will I handle that problem?"

There are going to be *plenty* of problems. The old way has been in place for centuries. Socrates complained about students being lazy and not paying attention. What I'm trying to do, in a quiet way, is to create a different approach to working with people—be it in the classroom, in the clinic, in the hospital, or in the family. As I point out in my book, control theory applies to all aspects of our lives. But the transition to control theory is going to be difficult.

Kappan: Why do you say that?

Glasser: During the last 50 or 75 years, we've tried all kinds of innovative approaches in education—but almost all of them have been based on stimulus/response psychology. We are now moving further and further into what I call the "identity society"—an affluent society in which most people are less concerned about bare survival and more concerned about their feelings of importance and their sense of belonging. At the same time, we are continuing to use stimulus/response psychology, which is antagonistic to those concerns.

The outcomes are easy to predict: fewer and fewer students will be actively involved in education, and alcohol and drug use (which gives the illusion of satisfaction) will increase. Unaware of control theory, people in power continue to say, "Push them harder; our concern is not what satisfies them, but what satisfies us." Control theory provides an alternative to this outmoded approach.

> **Telling students to "just say no" is not enough. Students have to know what the choices are so that, when they say no, they can also say yes to something better.**

Kappan: What advice would you give educators who wish to implement control theory in their schools?

Glasser: I propose a three-pronged implementation program: 1) teach control theory to teachers, 2) implement learning teams and other control-theory approaches in the classroom, and 3) teach students control theory, starting in kindergarten. Teach students that they have needs, that they're always trying to satisfy those needs, and that, when they behave well or badly in the classroom, those are *choices* that they are making in an attempt to satisfy their needs.

I'm currently producing a drug education program for schools that will teach students about control theory, so that they know they have choices. Telling students to "just say no" is not enough. Students have to know what the choices are so that, when they say no, they can also say yes to something better. In my experience, students can learn control theory, and they get very excited about it. If the teaching begins in kindergarten or first grade, students can actually begin to use control theory in their own lives well before they enter junior high school.

Kappan: That's an interesting point. Meanwhile, what kinds of assignments would a teacher who uses learning teams have to devise?

And would those assignments differ radically from what teachers are doing in classrooms today?

Glasser: Yes, I think that they would. There's no point in assembling a team of students and then telling that team to answer the questions at the end of the chapter. Students can complete an assignment of that sort individually. If a teacher gave a learning team such an assignment, a couple of students would answer the questions, and the others would hitchhike along without really becoming involved. It's as if the basketball coach, knowing John to be a crack shot, didn't bother to set up plays to get the ball to John.

By way of analogy, a teacher might say to a team of four students, "Here are four 50-pound sacks of cement. Will you, as a team, move them outside?" Let's assume that the team includes one big, strong boy. So the others say to him, "You're big and strong. You move the sacks outside." And he's a nice person, so he moves them, while the other members of the team just sit there.

What is needed instead is a *team* assignment, one that can't be completed unless the team works together. A team assignment would require the team to move a 200-pound sack of cement. One student couldn't budge it alone. To move the sack outside, the team would have to work together.

There are a variety of ways to set up good team assignments. My book provides several examples of such assignments—academic tasks that cannot be accomplished adequately by an individual student. A good team assignment also causes students to *want* to work together, because they perceive that together they can do a great job, but independently they can do very little.

Kappan: If a teacher is interested in trying the learning team approach, how should he or she get started?

Glasser: Teachers can start on their own, reading about learning teams and maybe observing a teacher who is experienced in the use of such teams. Later on, some formal training would probably be helpful—and such training is widely available.

A teacher could start independently, but that teacher would find it easier and more fun to work with a group of colleagues who want to try learning teams in their classrooms. Learning with others is not only in the spirit of the model; it *is* the model. A learning team of teachers could start by discussing control theory and trying to understand how it applies to them and to their students. Later on, the teachers could work together to plan good team assignments, and they could actually begin to use learning teams in their classrooms. As other teachers in the building see the new model at work, many of them will also begin to use learning teams.

Kappan: Do learning teams change the way teachers relate to their students?

Glasser: Of course. I've asked a lot of teachers who don't use learning teams, "How many students are actively involved with you in the learning process?" They tend to respond: "Six," "Eight," "Ten." The number doesn't matter. On their own, these students have formed their own little team. They may still function as individuals, but they get involved in discussions, and they ask the questions. Some of the other students are involved in learning, as well—but about half of the students in every class are not. The teacher doesn't get to know those students, and they feel unimportant.

> As the teacher moves from team to team, spending several minutes with each, the teacher gets to know those students.

When the teacher puts the uninvolved students on learning teams, things change, however. As the teacher moves from team to team, spending several minutes with each, the teacher gets to know those students. The teacher sits with them—at their level—and talks directly to them about academic matters. That gives the students a sense of belonging and a sense of importance.

Kappan: Is there any place in a learning-team classroom for large-group instruction?

Glasser: Oh, certainly. Lectures are fine, but teachers can't lecture 180 days a year. That's excessive. There are many creative ways to integrate lectures with learning teams, too. For example, in a 15- or 20-minute lecture, a teacher might supply the basic information about a project or a topic. Then that teacher might ask the students to sit down in learning teams to talk over the information and to raise questions.

I don't think that traditional teaching is 100% bad. Anything that works for 50% of the students in good schools can't be 100% bad. In good schools, though, lecturing is rarely the only approach that teachers use.

Kappan: You've talked a lot about cooperative learning and cooperative team assignments. What place does competition have in a classroom that uses the model of cooperative learning teams?

Glasser: Individual competition is intimidating, and most people shun it unless they believe they have a good chance to win. But human beings often compete as members of teams, and even when they lose, it's not as devastating. Moreover, individual competition is usually not fair. Some people are more gifted or more determined than others, and they're going to win every time. Teams make competition fairer, and, if one team wins too often, the teacher can redistribute its members.

Robert Slavin uses a lot of competition, especially with elementary students who are learning basic skills. Slavin encourages learning teams to compete with one another, and the students are highly motivated by such activities. They name their teams, form leagues, keep score—but Slavin makes sure that all teams have a chance to win.

Kappan: So you would recommend that teachers incorporate some competition at the team level?

Glasser: I think it's fun to compete, but much competition in this world is unfair. When horses race, the officials put more weight on the fastest horses to even the odds. In school, we tend to do the opposite; using poor grades as a handicap, we put more weight on the poor students and give more opportunities to the good ones. Naturally, the good students always win.

Learning teams, by contrast, give students a way to complete that is usually fair.

Kappan: If you had to distill the message of your new book, Control Theory in the Classroom, *into just a few sentences, what would those sentences be?*

> In control-theory schools, discipline problems will disappear, the number of teenage pregnancies will drop, drug use will diminish. . . .

Glasser: There is no doubt that knowledge is power, but U.S. schools aren't getting that message across. Most students do not see their schools as places that make them feel important—although that will happen in control-theory schools, as I have explained. In control-theory schools, discipline problems will disappear, the number of teenage pregnancies will drop, drug use will diminish—because all of these are self-destructive ways for young people to gain the sense of power and importance that they aren't finding today in their classrooms.

Kappan: Will implementing control theory in the classroom be costly?

Glasser: No, not at all. Schools are currently spending a disproportionate amount of money on what is, too often, a futile attempt to educate those students who choose not to work in school. Special programs have proliferated—especially programs for the "learning disabled," a group of students whose major disability is that they do not see school or education as need-satisfying.

In a control-theory school, this group would be substantially reduced. The resultant savings would be far larger than the small amount of money it would take to implement the program that I have suggested here. To get started, administrators need only begin to treat teachers as managers. That costs nothing and would benefit the educational system greatly, whether or not the rest of the program were ever put into place. Keep in mind, though, that students whose needs are satisfied learn more and cost less.

Caring Kids: The Role of the Schools

by Alfie Kohn

E ducation worthy of the name is essentially education of character," the philosopher Martin Buber told a gathering of teachers in 1939.[1] In saying this, he presented a challenge more radical and unsettling than his audience may have realized. He did not mean that schools should develop a unit on values or moral reasoning and glue it onto the existing curriculum. He did not mean that problem children should be taught how to behave. He meant that the very profession of teaching calls on us to try to produce not merely good learners but good people.

Given that even the more modest task of producing good learners seems impossibly ambitious—perhaps because of a misplaced emphasis on producing good test-takers—the prospect of taking Buber seriously may seem positively utopian. But in the half-century since his speech, the need for schools to play an active role in shaping character has only grown more pressing. That need is reflected not only in the much-cited prevalence of teenage pregnancy and drug use but also in the evidence of rampant selfishness and competitiveness among young people.* At a tender age, children learn not to be tender. A

> **The very profession of teaching calls on us to try to produce not merely good learners but good people.**

*Our society's current infatuation with the word *competitiveness*, which has leached into discussions about education, only exacerbates the problem by encouraging a confusion between two very different ideas: excellence and the desperate quest to triumph over other people.

From *Phi Delta Kappan,* vol. 72, no. 7, pp. 496–506, March 1991. © 1991 by Alfie Kohn. Reprinted with permission.

dozen years of schooling often do nothing to promote generosity or a commitment to the welfare of others. To the contrary, students are graduated who think that being smart means looking out for number one.

I want to argue, first, that something *can* be done to rectify the situation because nothing about "human nature" makes selfishness inevitable; second, that educators in particular *should* do something about the problem; and third, that psychological research, common sense, and the experience of an important pilot project in California offer specific guidance for helping children to grow into caring adults.

Much of what takes place in a classroom, including that which we have come to take for granted, emerges from a set of assumptions about the nature of human nature. Not only how children are disciplined, but the very fact that influencing their actions is viewed as "discipline" in the first place; not merely how we grade students, but the fact that we grade them at all; not simply how teachers and students interact, but the fact that the interaction *between students* is rarely seen as integral to the process of learning—all of these facts ultimately rest on an implicit theory of what human beings are like.

> Most conversations about changing the way children act in a classroom tend to focus on curbing negative behaviors rather than on promoting positive ones.

Consider the fact that most conversations about changing the way children act in a classroom tend to focus on curbing negative behaviors rather than on promoting positive ones. In part, this emphasis simply reflects the urgency of preventing troublesome or even violent conduct. But this way of framing the issue may also tell us something about our view of what comes naturally to children, what they are capable of, and, by extension, what lies at the core of our species. Likewise, it is no coincidence, I think, that the phrase "it's just human nature to be . . ." is invariably followed by such adjectives as selfish, competitive, lazy, aggressive, and so on. Very rarely do we hear someone protest, "Well, of course he was helpful. After all, it's just human nature to be generous."

The belief persists in this culture that our darker side is more pervasive, more persistent, and somehow more real than our capacity for what psychologists call "prosocial behavior." We seem to assume that people are naturally and primarily self-ish and will act otherwise only if they are coerced into doing so and carefully monitored. The logical conclusion of this world view is the assumption that generous and responsible behavior must be forced down the throats of children who would other-wise be inclined to care only about themselves.

A review of several hundred studies has convinced me that this cynicism is not realism. Human beings are not only selfish and self-centered, but also decent, able to feel—and prepared to try to relieve—the pain of others. I believe that it is as "natural" to help as it is to hurt, that concern for the well-being of others often cannot be reduced to self-interest, that social structures predicated on human selfishness have no claim to inevitabil-ity—or even prudence. This is not the place for rehearsing the arguments and data that support these conclusions—in part be-cause I have recently done so at book length.[2] But I would like to mention a few recent findings from developmental psychol-ogy that speak to the question of whether educators can aim higher than producing a quiet classroom or a nondisruptive child.

To start at the beginning, newborns are more likely to cry—and to cry longer—when they are exposed to the sound of another infant's crying than when they hear other noises that are equally loud and sudden. In three sets of studies with infants ranging in age from 18 to 72 hours, such crying seemed to be a spontaneous reaction rather than a mere vocal imitation.[3] In the view of Abraham Sagi and Martin Hoffman, who conducted one of the studies, this finding suggests the existence of "a rudi-mentary empathetic distress reaction at birth."[4] Our species may be primed, in other words, to be discomfited by someone else's discomfort.

As an infant grows, this discomfort continues and takes more sophisticated forms. Marian Radke-Yarrow, Carolyn Zahn-Waxler, and their associates at the National Institute of Mental Health have been studying toddlers for nearly 20 years, having in effect deputized mothers as research assistants to col-lect data in the home instead of relying on brief (and possibly

It is sometimes said that moral concerns and social skills ought to be taught at home. I know of no one in the field of education or child development who disagrees. The problem is that such instruction—along with nurturance and warmth, someone to model altruism, opportunities to practice caring for others, and so forth—is not to be found in all homes. The school may need to provide what some children will not otherwise get. In any case, there is no conceivable danger in providing these values in both environments. Encouragement from more than one source to develop empathic relationships is a highly desirable form of redundancy.

> **Encouragement from more than one source to develop empathic relationships is a highly desirable form of redundancy.**

The second concern one hears—and this one dovetails with the broader absence of interest in the prosocial realm—is the fear that children taught to care about others will be unable to look out for themselves when they are released into a heartless society. The idea that someone exposed to such a program will grow up gullible and spineless, destined to be victimized by mean-spirited individuals, can be traced back to the prejudice that selfishness and competitiveness are efficacious social strategies—a sterling example of what sociologist C. Wright Mills used to call "crackpot realism." In fact, those whose mantra is "look out for number one" are actually at a greater disadvantage in any sort of society than those who are skilled at working with others and inclined to do so. Competition and the single-minded pursuit of narrowly conceived self-interest typically turn out to be counterproductive.

By contrast, a well-designed program of prosocial instruction will include training in cooperative conflict resolution and in methods of achieving one's goals that do not require the use of force or manipulation. But even without such a component, there is nothing about caring for others that implies not caring for or looking after oneself. A raft of research has established that assertiveness, healthy self-esteem, and popularity are all compatible with—and often correlates of—a prosocial orientation.[9]

The final objection to teaching children to be caring individuals is that the time required to do so comes at the expense of attention to academics—a shift in priorities apt to be particularly unpopular at a time when we entertain ourselves by describing how much students don't know. In fact, though, there is absolutely no evidence to suggest that prosocial children—or the sort of learning experiences that help to create them—are mutually exclusive with academic achievement. To the contrary, the development of perspective-taking—the capacity to imagine how someone else thinks, feels, or sees the world—tends to promote cognitive problem solving generally. In one study, the extent to which girls had these skills at age 8 or 9 was a powerful predictor of performance on reading and spelling tests taken two years later—an even better predictor, in fact, than their original test scores.[10]

> **Hundreds of studies have shown that cooperative learning, which has an important place in a prosocial classroom, enhances achievement regardless of subject matter or age level.**

Not only are the ingredients of a prosocial orientation conducive to academic excellence, but the educational process itself does not require us to choose between teaching children to think and teaching them to care. It is possible to integrate prosocial lessons into the regular curriculum; as long as children are learning to read and spell and think critically, they may as well learn with texts that encourage perspective-taking. Indeed, to study literature or history by grappling with social and moral dilemmas is to invite a deeper engagement with those subjects. Meanwhile, literally hundreds of studies have shown that cooperative learning, which has an important place in a prosocial classroom, enhances achievement regardless of subject matter or age level.[11] So consistent and remarkable have these results been that schools and individual teachers often adopt models of cooperative learning primarily to strengthen academic performance. The development of prosocial values is realized as an unintended bonus.

Education of character in Buber's sense asks of teachers something more than the mere elimination of behavior problems in the classroom. The absence of such problems is often seen as an invitation to move past behavioral and social issues and get on with the business at hand, which is academic learning. I am arguing, by contrast, that behavioral and social issues, values and character, are very much part of the business at hand. But whether we are talking about addressing misconduct or about taking the initiative to help students become more responsive to one another, a teacher can take any of several basic orientations. Here are four approaches to changing behaviors and attitudes, presented in ascending order of desirability.

1. **Punishing.** A reliance on the threat of punishment is a reasonably good indication that something is wrong in a classroom, since children have to be bullied into acting the way the teacher demands. Apart from the disagreeable nature of this style of interaction—which cannot be disguised, incidentally, by referring to punishment as "consequences"—it is an approach distinguished mostly by its ineffectiveness. Decades of research have established that children subjected to punitive discipline at home are *more* likely than their peers to break rules when they are away from home.

Isolating a child from his peers, humiliating her, giving him an F, loading her with extra homework, or even threatening to do any of these things can produce compliance in the short run. Over the long haul, however, this strategy is unproductive.

Why? First, at best, punishment teaches nothing about what one is supposed to do—only about what one is not supposed to do. There is an enormous difference between not beating up one's peers, on the one hand, and being helpful, on the other.

Second, the child's attention is not really focused on the intended lesson at all ("pushing people is bad"), much less on the rationale for this principle, but primarily on the punishment itself. Figuring out how to get away with the misbehavior, how to avoid detection by an authority, is a perfectly logical response. (Notice that the one who punishes becomes transformed in the child's eyes into a rule-enforcer who is best avoided.) Social learning theory tells us that this attention to the punishment is also likely to *teach* the child to be punitive and thus exacerbate the behavior problems; a teacher's actions do indeed speak louder than words.

Finally, punishment breeds resistance and resentment. "The more you use power to try to control people, the less real influence you'll have on their lives," Thomas Gordon has written.[12] Since such influence is associated with helping children to develop good values, the use of power would seem ill-advised.

2. Bribing. There is no question that rewards are better than punishment. On the other hand, what these two methods share is probably more important than the respects in which they differ, and herein lies a tale that will be highly disconcerting to educators enamored of positive reinforcement. Psychological—and particularly developmental—theory and research have come a long way since the simplistic behaviorism of the last generation, but many well-meaning teachers continue to assume that what works for training the family pet must be appropriate for shaping children's actions and values as well.

> Not only is bribing someone to act in a particular way ultimately ineffective, but, like the use of threats, it can actually make things worse.

Gold stars, smiley faces, trophies, certificates, high grades, extra recess time, candy, money, and even praise all share the feature of being "extrinsic" to whatever behavior is being rewarded. Like sticks, carrots are artificial attempts to manipulate behavior that offer children *no reason to continue acting in the desired way when there is no longer any goody to be gained.* Do rewards motivate students? Absolutely. They motivate students to get rewarded. What they fail to do is help children develop a commitment to being generous or respectful.

In fact, the news is even worse than this. Not only is bribing someone to act in a particular way ultimately ineffective, but, like the use of threats, it can actually make things worse. Consider the effects of rewards on achievement. Yale psychologist Robert Sternberg recently summed up what a growing number of motivation researchers now concede: "Nothing tends to undermine creativity quite like extrinsic motivators do. They also undermine intrinsic motivation: when you give extrinsic rewards for certain kinds of behavior, you tend to reduce children's interest in performing those behaviors for their own sake."[13] Once we see ourselves as doing something in order to get a reward, we are less likely to want to continue doing it in the absence of a reward—even if we used to find it enjoyable.

Readers of the *Kappan* were first exposed to research demonstrating this phenomenon more than 15 years ago,[14] and the data have continued to accumulate since then, with some studies concentrating on how extrinsic motivators reduce intrinsic interest and others showing how they undermine performance, particularly on creative tasks.[15] A number of explanations have been proposed to account for these remarkably consistent findings. First, people who think of themselves as working for a reward feel controlled, and this lack of self-determination interferes with creativity. Second, rewards encourage "ego involvement" to the exclusion of "task involvement," and the latter is more predictive of achievement. Third, the promise of a reward is "tantamount to declaring that the activity is not worth doing for its own sake," as A. S. Neill put it;[16] indeed, anything construed as a prerequisite to some other goal will probably be devalued as a result.

> When someone is rewarded for prosocial behavior, that person will tend to assume that the reward accounts for his or her actions.

What is true for academic learning also applies to behavior. A little-known series of studies has pointed up the folly of trying to encourage prosocial behavior through the use of extrinsic incentives. Children who received rewards for donating to another child—and, in another experiment, adults who were paid for helping a researcher—turned out to be less likely to describe themselves in words suggesting intrinsic motivation to help than were people who received nothing in return.[17] In another study, women offered money for answering a questionnaire were less likely to agree to a similar request two or three days later, when no money was involved, than were women who had not been paid for helping with the first survey.[18]

The implication is that, when someone is rewarded for prosocial behavior, that person will tend to assume that the reward accounts for his or her actions and thus will be less likely to help once no one is around to hand out privileges or praise.

Indeed, elementary school students whose mothers believed in using rewards to motivate them were less cooperative and generous than other children in a recent study.[19] Such findings are of more than theoretical interest given the popularity of Skinnerian techniques for promoting generosity in schools. A recent *New York Times* article described elementary schools where helpful children have their pictures posted in hallways, get to eat at a special table in the cafeteria, or even receive money.[20] Such contrivances may actually have the effect of undermining the very prosocial orientation that their designers hope to promote.

3. Encouraging commitment to values. To describe the limitations of the use of punishments and rewards is already to suggest a better way: the teacher's goal should not be simply to produce a given behavior—for example, to get a child to share a cookie or stop yelling—but to help that child see himself or herself as the kind of person who is responsible and caring. From this shift in self-concept will come lasting behaviors and values that are not contingent on the presence of someone to dispense threats or bribes. The child has made these behaviors and values his or her own.

A student manipulated by currently fashionable behavioral techniques, however, is unlikely to internalize the values underlying the desired behaviors. At the heart of "assertive discipline," for example, is control: "I want teachers to learn that they have to take charge," Lee Canter explained recently.[21] I don't. I want *children* to become responsible for what they do and for what kind of people they are. The teacher has a critical role to play in making sure that this happens; in criticizing manipulative approaches I am not suggesting that children be left alone to teach themselves responsibility. But the teacher ought to be guided less by the need to maintain control over the classroom than by the long-term objective of helping students to act responsibly because they understand that it is right to do so.

I will have more to say below about strategies for facilitating this internalization, but first I want to mention a version of this process that I believe is even more desirable—the ideal approach to helping children become good people.

4. Encouraging the group's commitment to values. What the first two approaches have in common is that they provide nothing more than extrinsic motivation. What the first two share with the third is that they address only the individual child. I propose that helpfulness and responsibility ought not to be taught in a vacuum but in the context of a community of people who learn and play and make decisions together. More precisely, the idea is not just to internalize good values *in* a community but to internalize, among other things, the value *of* community.

> Helpfulness and responsibility ought not to be taught in a vacuum but in the context of a community of people who learn and play and make decisions together.

Perhaps the best way to crystallize what distinguishes each of these four approaches is to imagine the question that a child is encouraged to ask by each. An education based on punishment prompts the query, "What am I supposed to do, and what will happen to me if I don't do it?" An education based on rewards leads the child to ask, "What am I supposed to do, and what will I get for doing it?" When values have been internalized by the child, the question becomes "What kind of person do I want to be?" And, in the last instance, the child wonders: "How do we want our classroom (or school) to be?"

Educators eager to have children think about how they want their classrooms to be—which is to say, educators who do not feel threatened at the prospect of inviting children to share some of the responsibility for creating norms and determining goals—need to think in terms of five broad categories: what they believe, what they say, what they do, how they relate to students, and how they encourage students to relate to one another. Let us consider each in turn.

What educators believe. The famous Pygmalion effect refers to the fact that a teacher's assumptions about a child's intellectual potential can affect that child's performance. Such self-fulfilling prophecies, however, are by no means limited to academics; they also operate powerfully on a child's actions and values. Write off a student as destructive or disruptive, and he or she is likely to "live down to" these expectations. Conversely—and here is the decisive point for anyone concerned with promoting generosity—attributing to a child the best possible motive that is consistent with the facts may set in motion an "auspicious" (rather than a vicious) circle. We help students develop good values by assuming whenever possible that they are already motivated by these values—rather than by explaining an ambiguous action in terms of a sinister desire to make trouble.

However, what we assume about a given student is also colored by our assumptions regarding human nature itself. While I am not aware of any research on this question, it seems reasonable to suppose that an educator who thinks that self-interest motivates everything we do will be suspicious of individual instances of generosity. Someone who takes for granted that a Hobbesian state of nature would exist in a classroom in the absence of a controlling adult to keep children in line, who believes that children need to be leaned on or "taught a lesson" or bribed to act responsibly, is likely to transfer these expectations to the individual child and to produce an environment that fulfills them. The belief that children are actually quite anxious to please adults, that they may simply lack the skills to get what they need, that they will generally respond to a caring environment can create a very different reality. What you believe matters.

> **Pointing out how their actions affect others sensitizes students to the needs and feelings of others and tacitly communicates a message of trust and responsibility.**

What educators say. An immense body of research has shown that children are more likely to follow a rule if its rationale has been explained to them and that, in general, discipline based on reason is more effective than the totalitarian approach captured by the T-shirt slogan "Because I'm the mommy, that's why." This finding applies not only to discouraging aggression but to promoting altruism. From preschool to high school, children should learn why—not merely be told that—helping others is good. Pointing out how their actions affect others sensitizes students to the needs and feelings of others and tacitly communicates a message of trust and responsibility. It implies that, once children understand how their behavior makes other people feel, they can and will choose to do something about it.

How such explanations are framed also counts. First, the level of the discourse should be fitted to the child's ability to understand. Second, the concept of using reason does not preclude passion. A prohibition on hurting people, for example, should not be offered dispassionately but with an emotional charge to show that it matters. Third, prosocial activity should not be promoted on the basis of self-interest. "Zachary, if you don't share your dump truck with Linda, she won't let you play with her dinosaur" has an undeniable appeal for a parent, but it is a strategy more likely to inculcate self-regarding shrewdness than genuine concern for others. The same goes for classroom exhortations and instruction.

A series of studies by Joan Grusec of the University of Toronto and her colleagues is also relevant. Her research provides a concrete alternative to the use of rewards or praise to elicit generosity. "Children who view their prosocial conduct as compliance with external authority will act prosocially only when they believe external pressures are present," she has written. Far preferable is for children to "come to believe that their prosocial behavior reflects values or dispositions in themselves."[22]

This result is best achieved by verbally attributing such values or dispositions to the child. In one experiment, in which children gave away some of their game winnings after watching a model do so, those who were told that they had made the donation "because you're the kind of person who likes to help other people" were subsequently more generous than those who were told that they had donated because they were expected to do so.[23] In another study, the likelihood of children's donating increased both when they were praised and when they were led to think of themselves as helpful people. But in a follow-up experiment, it was the latter group who turned out to be more generous than those who had received verbal reinforcement. In other words, praise increased generosity in a given setting but ceased to be effective outside of that setting, whereas children with an intrinsic impulse to be generous continued to act on that motivation in other circumstances.[24]

A study of adults drives home the point. Subjects who were told that a personality test showed that they were kind and thoughtful people were more likely to help a confederate who "accidentally" dropped a pile of cards than were those who were told that they were unusually intelligent or those given no feedback at all. This finding is important because it implies that being led to think of oneself as generous does not affect behavior merely because it is a kind of reinforcement or a mood-enhancer; this label apparently encourages prosocial action because it helps to build a view of the self as altruistic.

This is not to suggest that a teacher's every utterance must be—or can be—applied toward internalization. Simply making sure that a classroom is a safe environment conducive to learning can require the sort of behavioral interventions on a day-to-day basis that don't do much to strengthen a child's prosocial self-concept. But the more teachers attend to the latter, the fewer problems they are likely to have over the long run.

What educators do. Children of all ages, from before the time they can read until after the time they start seeking distance from adults, learn from what they see. Studies show that children who watched, even briefly, as someone donated to charity were themselves likely to donate more than other children—even if months had elapsed since the exposure to the model.[26] The extent to which a teacher expresses concern about people in distress and takes the initiative to help—which applies both to how the teacher treats the students themselves and how he or she refers to people outside the classroom—can set a powerful example and be even more effective than didactic instruction in promoting a sense of caring in students.

> The extent to which a teacher expresses concern about people in distress and takes the initiative to help . . . can set a powerful example.

There is no shortage of suggestions about how to devise lessons that address social and ethical issues, ranging from explicit training in perspective-taking or moral reasoning to discussions about values that can, in turn, include either "clarification" of the beliefs that students already hold or old fashioned lectures on character or morality. Most of the debate on the subject occurs between proponents of just such programs, each accusing the other of being relativistic or of seeking to indoctrinate. Far less consideration is given to the possibility of integrating such issues into the regular curriculum.

kens to a stranger than were those who studied on their own; in another, kindergartners who participated in cooperative activities acted more prosocially than their peers in a traditional classroom.[29] But the consequences are not limited to generosity per se. Carefully structured cooperative learning also promotes a subjective sense of group identity, a greater acceptance of people who are different from oneself (in terms of ethnicity or ability level), and a more sophisticated ability to imagine other people's points of view.[30] Cooperation is an essentially humanizing experience that predisposes participants to take a benevolent view of others. It allows them to transcend egocentric and objectifying postures and encourages trust, sensitivity, open communication, and prosocial activity.

Second, teachers can move the idea of discipline not only away from punishments and rewards but also away from the premise of these strategies—namely, that teachers should simply be figuring out by themselves how to elicit compliance with a set of rules or goals that they alone devise. The realistic alternative is not for the teacher to abdicate responsibility for what happens in the classroom but rather to bring in (and guide) children so that they can play a role in making decisions about how their classroom is to be run and why. (Must hands always be raised or only during certain kinds of discussions? What is the best way for the class as a community to balance principles of fairness and the spontaneity that encourages participation?)

Discipline would thus be reconfigured as collaborative planning and mutual problem solving. Such an approach will be preferred by anyone who favors the idea of autonomy and democratic decision making—but it can also be argued that purely practical considerations recommend it, since children are more likely to follow rules that they have helped to create than rules dictated to them. This, of course, assumes that following rules is in itself a desirable goal. More broadly, educators need to ask themselves and each other about the ultimate objective of discipline. Even if one of the conventional programs of behavior control succeeded in keeping children quiet, do quiet children learn more effectively or merely make fewer demands on the teacher? (The Johnsons like to say that a principal walking through the school corridors should be concerned if he or she hears no sound coming from a classroom; this means that real learning probably is not taking place.) And which approach is most likely to help children come to care about one another?

To invite children to participate in making decisions not only about classroom procedures but also about pedagogical matters (what is to be learned, how, and why) and housekeeping matters (how to celebrate birthdays or decorate the walls) is to bring them into a process of discussion, an opportunity to cooperate and build consensus. To this extent, it is a chance for them to practice perspective-taking skills, to share and listen and help. In short, involving children in planning and decision making is a way of providing a framework for prosocial interactions that supports other such opportunities; it turns a routine issue into another chance to learn about and practice caring—and, not so incidentally, thinking as well.[31]

> Involving children in planning and decision making is a way of providing a framework for prosocial interactions.

Finally, educators can provide students with opportunities to be responsible for one another so that they will learn (prosocial values and skills) by doing. Ideally, this can include interaction with those of different ages. For an older child to guide someone younger is to experience firsthand what it is to be a helper and to be responsible for someone who is dependent on him or her. For the younger child, this cross-age interaction presents an opportunity to see a prosocial model who is not an adult.

One of the most exciting and innovative educational programs now in operation, the Child Development Project (CDP), is devoted specifically to helping children become more caring and responsible.[32] The experience of the CDP offers lessons in the systematic application of many of the ideas discussed here; indeed, I owe my formulation of some of these ideas to the work done by Eric Schaps, Marilyn Watson, and others involved with the project.

The CDP is the first long-term, comprehensive, school-based project in prosocial education. After being invited a decade ago to work in the Sam Ramon Valley (California) Unified School District, about 30 miles east of San Francisco, the staff carefully matched two sets of three elementary schools in the district for size and socioeconomic status. A coin flip then determined which of these sets would receive the program and which would serve as the comparison group. The first teachers were trained before the start of the 1982–83 school year. Staff researchers focused on a group of children in the experimental schools (then in kindergarten and now in junior high school) to assess whether their attitudes, behavior, and achievement differed significantly from those of their counterparts in the comparison schools. In the fall of 1988, the program was introduced into two elementary schools in nearby Hayward, a district more ethnically diverse than the white, affluent suburbs in San Ramon Valley, and Schaps is now seeking funding to take the program to eight more sites around the country.

"How do we want our classroom to be?" is exactly the question that the CDP would have children ask. Rejecting punishment and rewards in favor of strategies geared toward internalization of prosocial norms and values, the CDP invites teachers and students to work together to turn their classrooms into caring communities. The primary components of the program intended to bring this about are these:

• a version of cooperative learning that does not rely on grades or other extrinsic motivators;

• the use of a literature-based reading program that stimulates discussion about values and offers examples of empathy and caring even as it develops verbal skills;

• an approach to classroom management in which the emphasis is on developing intrinsic motives to participate productively and prosocially, in which teachers are encouraged to develop warm relationships with the children, and in which periodic class meetings are held so that children can play an active role in planning, assessing progress, and solving problems; and

• a variety of other features, including pairing children of different ages to work together, setting up community service projects to develop responsibility, giving periodic homework assignments specifically designed to be done (and to foster communication) with parents, and holding schoolwide activities that may involve whole families.

In their writings, members of the CDP staff have distinguished their way of teaching values from the approaches of better-known models. Unlike certain kinds of character education, the CDP approach emphasizes helping students understand the reason for a given value rather than simply insisting that they accept it or behave in a certain way because they have been told to do so. Unlike purely child-centered approaches, however, the CDP is committed to the importance of adult socialization: the teacher's job is to teach, to guide, to enforce, to facilitate cooperation, to model behaviors—in short, to be much more than a passive bystander. Prosocial values come from a synthesis of adult inculcation and peer interaction, and these values—in contrast to the programs developed by some theorists in the area of moral reasoning—emphasize caring for others as well as applying principles of fairness.

> **Prosocial values come from a synthesis of adult inculcation and peer interaction, and these values . . . emphasize caring for others as well as applying principles of fairness.**

Prior to the implementation of the CDP, students randomly selected from the three experimental and the three comparison schools proved to be similar not only demographically but also on a range of social attitudes, values, and skills. Once the program was implemented, however, structured interviews and observations turned up significant differences between students participating in the program and those in the comparison schools on some, though not all, measures.

Children taking part in the CDP engaged in a greater number of spontaneous prosocial behaviors in class, seemed better able to understand hypothetical conflict situations, and were more likely to take everyone's needs into account in dealing with such situations. They were more likely to believe that one has an obligation to speak up in a discussion even if one's position seems unlikely to prevail (which should answer those concerned about the assertiveness of caring children). While the CDP's emphasis has not required any sacrifice of conventional achievement (as measured by standardized test scores), neither has it given participants a consistent academic advantage over students in comparison schools. (In part, this finding may be due to a ceiling effect: students in the district already score in the top 10% of California schoolchildren, so there is not much room for improvement.) By the time the CDP group reached sixth grade, though, they were outscoring their counterparts in the comparison schools on a measure of higher-order reading comprehension (essays written about stories and poems).

It remains to be seen whether and in what ways the values and behaviors of children from schools using the CDP will continue to distinguish them from those who attended comparison schools now that they are all in junior high school. But this pilot project provides real evidence for the larger point I am making here: it is both realistic and valuable to attend to what students learn in the classroom about getting along with their peers. Children can indeed be raised to work with, care for, and help one another. And schools must begin to play an integral role in that process.

NOTES

1. Martin Buber, *Between Man and Man,* trans. Ronald Gregor Smith (New York: Macmillan, 1965), p. 104.

2. Alfie Kohn, *The Brighter Side of Human Nature: Altruism and Empathy in Everyday Life* (New York: Basic Books, 1990).

3. Marvin L. Simner, "Newborn's Response to the Cry of Another Infant," *Developmental Psychology,* vol. 5, 1971, pp. 136–50; Abraham Sagi and Martin L. Hoffman, "Empathic Distress in the Newborn," *Developmental Psychology,* vol. 12, 1976, pp. 175–76; and Grace B. Martin and Russell D. Clark III, "Distress Crying in Neonates: Species and Peer Specificity," *Developmental Psychology,* vol. 18, 1982, pp. 3–9.

4. Sagi and Hoffman, p. 176.

5. See, for example, Carolyn Zahn-Waxler and Marian Radke-Yarrow, "The Development of Altruism: Alternative Research Strategies," in Nancy Eisenberg-Berg, ed., *The Development of Prosocial Behavior* (New York: Academic Press, 1982).

6. Marian Radke-Yarrow and Carolyn Zahn-Waxler, "Dimensions and Correlates of Prosocial Behavior in Young Children," *Child Development,* vol. 47, 1976, pp. 118–25.

7. Nancy Eisenberg-Berg and Cynthia Neal, "Children's Moral Reasoning About Their Own Spontaneous Prosocial Behavior," *Developmental Psy-*

chology, vol. 15, 1979, pp. 228–29. Eisenberg and another colleague have observed that appeals to authority or punishment (which were completely absent here) are what one would expect if the children were at Lawrence Kohlberg's first stage of moral reasoning and that the apparently altruistic needs-oriented explanations have often—and presumably unfairly—been coded as stage 2, that is, as an immature, "preconventional" way of thinking about moral problems (see Nancy Eisenberg-Berg and Michael Hand, "The Relationship of Preschoolers' Reasoning About Prosocial Moral Conflicts to Prosocial Behavior," *Child Development*, vol. 50, 1979, pp. 356–63).

8. The tendency to define *altruism* so narrowly that only Mother Teresa would qualify for the label both reflects and perpetuates a cynical view of human nature. It would never occur to us to define *aggression* so as to exclude everything short of mass murder.

9. Kohn, Ch. 3.

10. Norma Deitch Feshbach and Seymour Feshbach, "Affective Processes and Academic Achievement," *Child Development*, vol. 58, 1987, pp. 1335–47. For more research on cognitive skills and perspective-taking, see David W. Johnson and Frank P. Johnson, *Joining Together: Group Theory and Group Skills*, 3rd ed. (Englewood Cliffs, N.J.: Prentice-Hall, 1987), p. 244.

11. For example, see David Johnson et al., "Effects of Cooperative, Competitive, and Individualistic Goal Structures on Achievement: A Meta-Analysis," *Psychological Bulletin*, vol. 89, 1981, pp. 47–62; David W. Johnson and Roger T. Johnson, *Cooperation and Competition* (Edina, Minn.: Interaction Book Co., 1989), especially Ch. 3; and Robert E. Slavin, *Cooperative Learning: Theory, Research, and Practice* (Englewood Cliffs, N.J.: Prentice-Hall, 1990), especially Ch. 2.

12. Thomas Gordon, *Teaching Children Self-Discipline* (New York: Times Books, 1989), p. 7.

13. Robert J. Sternberg, "Prototypes of Competence and Incompetence," in Robert J. Sternberg and John Kolligian, Jr., eds., *Competence Considered* (New Haven: Yale University Press, 1990), p. 144.

14. Mark R. Lepper and David Greene, "When Two Rewards Are Worse Than One: Effects of Extrinsic Rewards on Intrinsic Motivation," *Phi Delta Kappan*, April 1975, pp. 565–66.

15. See, for example, Edward Deci and Richard Ryan, *Intrinsic Motivation and Self-Determination in Human Behavior* (New York: Plenum Press, 1985); Mark R. Lepper and David Greene, eds., *The Hidden Costs of Reward* (Hillsdale, N.J.: Erlbaum, 1978); and the work of John Nicholls, Teresa Amabile, Judith M. Harackiewicz, Mark Morgan, and Ruth Butler. I have reviewed some of this research in "Group Grade Grubbing Versus Cooperative *Learning*," *Educational Leadership*, February 1991, pp. 83–87.

16. Quoted in Mark Morgan, "Reward-Induced Decrements and Increments in Intrinsic Motivation," *Review of Educational Research*, vol. 54, 1984, p. 5.

17. Cathleen L. Smith et al., "Children's Causal Attributions Regarding Help Giving," *Child Development*, vol. 50, 1979, p. 203–10; and C. Daniel Batson et al., "Buying Kindness: Effect of an Extrinsic Incentive for Helping on Perceived Altruism," *Personality and Social Psychology Bulletin*, vol. 4, 1978, pp. 86–91.

18. Miron Zuckerman, Michelle M. Lazzaro, and Diane Waldgeir, "Undermining Effects of the Foot-in-the-Door Technique with Extrinsic Rewards," *Journal of Applied Social Psychology*, vol. 9, 1979, pp. 292–96.

19. Richard A. Fabes et al., "Effects of Rewards on Children's Prosocial Motivation," *Developmental Psychology*, vol. 25, 1989, pp. 509–15.

20. Suzanne Daley, "Pendulum Is Swinging Back to the Teaching of Values in U. S. Schools," *New York Times*, 12 December 1990, p. B-14.

21. Quoted in David Hill, "Order in the Classroom," *Teacher Magazine*, April 1990, p. 77.

22. Joan E. Grusec and Theodore Dix, "The Socialization of Prosocial Behavior: Theory and Reality," in Carolyn Zahn-Waxler, E. Mark Cummings, and Ronald Iannotti, eds., *Altruism and Aggression: Biological and Social Origins* (Cambridge: Cambridge University Press, 1986), p. 220.

23. Joan E. Grusec et al., "Modeling, Direct Instruction, and Attributions: Effects on Altruism," *Developmental Psychology*, vol. 14, 1978, pp. 51–57.

24. Joan E. Grusec and Erica Redler, "Attribution, Reinforcement, and Altruism: A Developmental Analysis," *Developmental Psychology*, vol. 16, 1980, pp. 525–34.

25. Angelo Strenta and William DeJong, "The Effect of a Prosocial Label on Helping Behavior," *Social Psychology Quarterly*, vol. 44, 1981, pp. 142–47.

26. See James H. Bryan and Nancy H. Walbek, "Preaching and Practicing Generosity," *Child Development*, vol. 41, 1970, pp. 329–53; James H. Bryan and Perry London, "Altruistic Behavior by Children," *Psychological Bulletin*, vol. 72, 1970, pp. 200–211; Martin L. Hoffman, "Altruistic Behavior and the Parent-Child Relationship," *Journal of Personality and Social Psychology*, vol. 31, 1975, pp. 937–43; and Marian Radke-Yarrow, Phyllis M. Scott, and Carolyn Zahn-Waxler, "Learning Concern for Others," *Developmental Psychology*, vol. 8, 1973, pp. 240–60.

27. Ben Spiecker, "Psychopathy: The Incapacity to Have Moral Emotions," *Journal of Moral Education*, vol. 17, 1988, p. 103.

28. For an analysis of the harms of competition in the classroom and elsewhere, see Alfie Kohn, *No Contest: The Case Against Competition* (Boston: Houghton Mifflin, 1986).

29. David W. Johnson et al., "Effects of Cooperative Versus Individualized Instruction on Student Prosocial Behavior, Attitudes Toward Learning, and Achievement," *Journal of Educational Psychology*, vol. 68, 1976, pp. 446–52; and Bette Chambers, "Cooperative Learning in Kindergarten:

Can It Enhance Students' Perspective-Taking Ability and Prosocial Behavior?," unpublished manuscript, Concordia University, Montreal, 1990.

30. See, for example, the research cited in David W. Johnson and Roger T. Johnson, "The Socialization and Achievement Crisis: Are Cooperative Learning Experiences the Solution?," in Leonard Bickman, ed., *Applied Social Psychology Annual 4* (Beverly Hills, Calif.: Sage, 1983), p. 137; and Elliot Aronson and Diane Bridgeman, "Jigsaw Groups and the Desegregated Classroom: In Pursuit of Common Goals," *Personality and Social Psychology Bulletin*, vol. 5, 1979, p. 443.

31. Another classroom management issue is raised by Carolyn Zahn-Waxler. She warns that a teacher who routinely and efficiently takes care of a child in distress in order to preserve order in the classroom may unwittingly be teaching two lessons: (1) that "people do not react emotionally to upset in others," and (2) that "if someone is hurt, someone else who is in charge will handle it" ("Conclusions: Lessons from the Past and a Look to the Future," in Zahn-Waxler, Cummings, and Iannotti, p. 310).

32. For more about the Child Development Project, see Alfie Kohn, "The ABC's of Caring," *Teacher Magazine*, January 1990, pp. 52–58; and idem, *The Brighter Side of Human Nature*, Ch. 6. For accounts written by members of the staff, see Victor Battistich et al., "The Child Development Project: A Comprehensive Program for the Development of Prosocial Character," in William M. Kurtines and Jacob L. Gewirtz, eds., *Moral Behavior and Development: Advances in Theory, Research, and Applications* (Hillsdale, N. J.: Erlbaum, 1989); and Daniel Solomon et al., "Cooperative Learning as Part of a Comprehensive Classroom Program Designed to Promote Prosocial Development," in Shlomo Sharan, ed., *Cooperative Learning: Theory and Research* (New York: Praeger, 1990).

Establishing the Climate for an Interactive Classroom

Resesarchers have been generating volumes of data on effective schools and effective teachers. Their studies indicate that certain teaching techniques lead to better learning and better behavior.

—Thomas R. McDaniel

A sound educational philosophy built on research and theory is the foundation for effective classroom management. However, a teacher, especially a new teacher, needs more than a pedagogical theory book when thirty-two third graders come storming through the door the first day of school in September. This teacher better have some sturdy floor boards to support his or her philosophical base, or the foundation could crack and maybe collapse by October. Studies conducted at all grade levels have found that effective teachers begin the school year with a plan. They establish their management system the minute the students walk through the door. Moreover, they continuously monitor and reinforce the system and revise it as needed throughout the year.

Effective teachers clearly explain and integrate their classroom procedures, rules, and consequences into a workable system whereby students are introduced to procedures as needed, get a chance to practice them, and feel comfortable and secure with them. Ineffective teachers, on the other hand, introduce all their rules and procedures the first day and do not allow students time to understand or practice them, or they adopt a type of "we'll see if we need rules later" philosophy whereby students do not know what is expected of them. In these classrooms, students often interrupt the flow of instruction by walking around the room asking questions or disrupting others. The classroom climate does not provide the expectations, consistency, and structure that many students need in school because they lack structure in their home life.

When the situation becomes too chaotic, as it often does in the first weeks of school, the ineffective teacher may try to introduce some parameters to reestablish classroom decorum and regain his or her sanity. Alas, it is often too late since students have already been conditioned to the helter-skelter atmosphere that is sometimes masquerading in the guise of "giving students freedom and responsibility to make their own choices."

Student empowerment and curriculum choice are important in the cooperative classroom, but teachers need to set the parameters and establish the guidelines within which students can make some "educated" choices. Burke and McDaniel offer some principles and tips for helping teachers establish a positive classroom climate that sets high expectations the first day of class. Students are taught how to assume personal responsibility, exercise leadership skills, and make choices within the boundaries established by the class, the teacher, the principal, and the school system.

Laying the Groundrules for the School Year

by Kay Burke

I feel it is very important that we always walk in the halls and enter the room slowly. Why do you think that procedure is important?" asks Mrs. Saunders.

"I saw a boy get hurt once when another boy was rushing into the room and knocked him into the doorknob real hard," Mary replies.

"I don't like getting shoved by someone who is afraid of being late," adds John.

"So, you think we should all be courteous and enter the room walking rather than running or shoving?" Mrs. Saunders asks.

"Yes," says the class.

"All right, let's practice how we should enter the room. Everyone file out quietly and stand by the drinking fountain down the hall. When I give the signal, you will all walk toward our classroom and enter the room the way we discussed."

Students rehearse entering the classroom and taking their seat.

"I really liked the way you took turns entering the room and going to your desks. Now, what do you think would be a consequence if someone forgot our procedure and ran into someone while running into the room?"

"I think that person should have to go back and practice walking into the room again just like we practiced today," says Juan.

"He should also have to apologize to whoever he ran into 'cause no one likes to be pushed," Jack adds.

"Okay," says Mrs. Saunders, "I think we all agree on the importance of this procedure. We'll add this to our list of classroom procedures and consequences."

Adapted from *What to Do with the Kid Who . . .: Developing Cooperation, Self-Discipline, and Responsibility in the Classroom*, pp. 7–19, 30–35. © 1992 by IRI/Skylight Training and Publishing. All rights reserved.

THE NEED FOR STRUCTURE

Very few students function well in a chaotic environment. Even though students may pretend to like the freedom to do whatever they want, whenever they want, most of them prefer structures or routines so they know exactly what they are supposed to do.

Teachers can be creative and structure open-ended cooperative activities that allow students lots of options and choices. However, students need to "walk" before they can "run," and it is essential that they know their boundaries the first week of class. Teachers should prepare a tentative list of procedures they feel are necessary for establishing routines that are essential for the organization of the classroom; however, the entire class should discuss the rationale for the procedures and have some input in their final adoption.

The most effective way to handle discipline problems is to prevent them. The proactive teacher anticipates potential management problems and establishes a positive classroom environment where students feel secure because they know what is expected of them.

Researchers in the area of classroom management offer the following tips for teachers:

1. Proactive teachers take actions to try to prevent discipline problems.

2. Students who are actively involved in the learning process cause fewer behavior problems.

3. Teachers who use instructional time efficiently have fewer management problems.

Good classroom management is primarily *prevention*, not intervention, *planning* before the year begins, *implementing* on the first day of school, and *maintaining* consistently throughout the year. "Procedures are ways of getting class activities done. Their function is to routinize tasks for continuity, predictability, and time saving" (Evertson and Harris 1991, 2). They recommend four steps in teaching classroom procedures:

1. Explain.
   a. give concrete definition of procedures
   b. provide the reason or rationale
   c. demonstrate the procedure

d.   present the task step by step
e.   explain and demonstrate cues
2. Rehearse the procedure.
3. Provide feedback to individuals and the class.
4. Reteach procedures as necessary.

The procedures in a class should relate to the important principles that permeate the classroom climate. If students are expected to be prepared, on time, courteous, and respectful of others' rights, the procedures should support those principles. Courteous and responsible behavior builds cooperation and teamwork. Students feel obliged to treat other students the way they would like to be treated.

Teachers need to decide on the types of procedures that will be needed for their students and be prepared to discuss the procedures during the first few days of school. Some procedures may be *negotiable,* and some procedures will be *nonnegotiable.* Some of the procedures may also have consequences if they are violated. The teacher and the students should discuss the necessity of the procedures offered by the teacher, vote on their adoption, and post them in the room.

Many of the procedures should be rehearsed or role-played, and the teacher should gently remind students of the procedures by standing close to a student and pointing to the list of procedures posted in the room.

The key to effective procedures is consistency. If a procedure isn't working, discuss it and change it. But if the procedure is necessary and it is on the list, enforce it. The breakdown in classroom management doesn't usually start with a bang—it starts with a whimper!

CLASSROOM PROCEDURES: DO STUDENTS KNOW WHAT IS EXPECTED OF THEM FOR ROUTINE OPERATIONS?

Prepare a list of procedures you think are necessary to perform routine operations and present it to the students for discussion. The procedures will vary depending on the age level of the students. Check the categories in Figure 1 that apply to your situation and then prepare your list.

Figure 1
Classroom Procedures

A. **Beginning the Class**
   - ❏ How should students enter the room?
   - ❏ What constitutes being late (in the room, in the seat)?
   - ❏ How and when will absentee slips be handled?
   - ❏ What type of seating arrangements will be used (assigned seats, open seating, cooperative group seating)?
   - ❏ How will students get materials (materials manager in group, first student in each row, designated person)?
   - ❏ How will the teacher get students' attention to start class (the tardy bell, raised hand, lights turned off and on)?

B. **Classroom Management**
   - ❏ How and when will students leave their seats?
   - ❏ What do students need in order to leave the room (individual passes, room pass, teacher's permission)?
   - ❏ How will students get help from teacher (raised hand, put name on board, ask other group members first)?
   - ❏ What are acceptable noise levels for discussion, group work, seat work?
   - ❏ How should students work with other students (moving desks, changing seats, noise level, handling materials)?
   - ❏ How will students get recognized to talk (raised hand, teacher calls on student, talk out)?

C. **Paper Work**
   - ❏ How will students turn in work (put in specific tray or box, pass to the front, one student collects)?
   - ❏ How will students turn in make-up work if they were absent (special tray, give to the teacher, put in folder, give to teacher's aide)?
   - ❏ How will students distribute handouts (first person in row, a group member gets a copy for all group members, students pick up as they enter room)?
   - ❏ How will late work be graded (no penalty, minus points, zero, "F," use lunch or recess to finish, turn in by end of day, lowered letter grade)?
   - ❏ How and when will students make up quizzes and tests missed (same day they return to school, within twenty-

four hours, within the week, before school, during lunch or recess, after school)?

❏ How will late projects such as research papers, portfolios, and artwork will be graded (no penalty, minus points, lowered letter grade, no late work accepted)?

D. **Dismissal from Class or School**

❏ When do students leave class for the day (when bell rings, when teacher gives the signal)?

❏ Can students stay after class to finish assignments, projects, tests?

❏ Can the teacher keep one student or the whole class after class or school?

E. **Syllabus or Course Outline**

❏ How are students made aware of course objectives?

❏ How are students made aware of course requirements?

❏ Are students given due dates for major assignments several weeks in advance?

❏ Are students told how they will be evaluated and given the grading scale?

F. **Other Procedures**

(You may need to introduce procedures related to recess, assemblies, guest speakers, substitute teachers, field trips, fire drills, teacher leaving room, etc.)

THE "GOLDEN" RULES

If classroom procedures form the framework for a climate conducive to students and teachers working together cooperatively, the classroom rules form the heart and soul of caring, cooperative classrooms. If students are going to "buy into" the system, they must be a part of the process.

According to Kohn (1991), "an immense body of research has shown that children are more likely to follow a rule if its rationale has been explained to them. . . . Discipline based on reason is more effective than the totalitarian approach captured by the T-shirt slogan 'Because I'm the Mommy, that's why'"
(p. 502).

Curwin and Mendler (1988) feel that effective rules describe specific behavior. They also believe that effective rules should be built on principles like honesty, courtesy, helpfulness, and the like. Evertson and Harris (1991, 2) offer eight guidelines for writing classroom rules.

Rules should be . . .

1. Consistent with school rules
2. Understandable
3. Doable (students able to comply)
4. Manageable
5. Always applicable (consistent)
6. Stated positively
7. Stated behaviorally
8. Consistent with teacher's own philosophy of how students learn best

Clearly stated rules that describe specific behavior enable students to understand what is expected of them. If rules are too specific, however, too many rules will be needed.

Too general: "Student shouldn't bother other students."
Too specific: "Students should not grab, push, shove, or trip other students."
Better rule: "It is best that students keep their hands off other people."

It is imperative that students get an opportunity to discuss the proposed classroom rules and understand the rationale behind the rules. A class meeting is the perfect opportunity to have a frank discussion of the rules, to role-play situations, and to come to a class consensus about the rules the students and teacher will adopt in order to ensure a positive, organized classroom environment.

It is important to note again that some rules are nonnegotiable. Students must understand that the school district or the school itself sets down some rules that are not subject to a vote. Rules related to fighting, damage to property, injury to self or others are absolute; therefore, they set parameters for all students in order to ensure their health and safety.

After the class members and teacher have come to a consensus on their classroom rules, they should discuss and agree on the logical consequences students will face if they violate the rules. The old-fashioned "punishment" paradigm is not effective. As Kohn (1991) states, "reliance on the threat of punishment is a reasonably good indication that something is wrong in a classroom, since children have to be bullied into acting the way the teacher demands" (p. 500).

If teachers are to establish an atmosphere of cooperation where students assume responsibility for their actions, the old obedience model of "spare the rod, spoil the child" is ineffectual. Kohn (1991) notes that "isolating a child from his peers, humiliating her, giving him an F, loading her with extra homework, or even threatening to do any of these things can produce compliance in the short run. Over the long run, however, this strategy is unproductive" (p. 500).

TRUTH OR CONSEQUENCES

Consequences, on the other hand, relate directly to the rule violation and seem more logical and just than punishments. Curwin and Mendler (1988) warn, however, that "a consequence can become a punishment if it is delivered aggressively" (p. 65). According to Curwin and Mendler consequences work best when they . . .

1. are clear and specific.
2. have a range of alternatives.
   a. reminder
   b. warning [or second reminder]
   c. conference with student
   d. conference with parent and/or administrator
3. are not punishments.
4. are natural and/or logical.
5. are related to the rule.

For example, if a student violates the rule about homework by not completing it, the consequence would not logically be to send that student to the principal. The consequence would more logically involve having the student turn in the homework before the end of the day, stay in from recess or lunch to finish it, or lose points. Consequences relate directly to the rule violation. Across-the-board punishments such as "sit in the corner," "go to the office," or "miss the field trip" are punitive.

Punishment often diminishes the dignity of the student as well as breeds resentment and resistance. Kohn (1991) says that punishment teaches nothing about what a student is supposed to do—only about what he is not supposed to do. Curwin and Mendler (1988) feel that if students are only motivated by a reward-and-punishment system, they will only behave out of fear of getting caught rather than out of a sense of social responsibility. And Glasser (1990) warns that students will not be coerced into doing anything. They must see the rationale behind the rules, and they must be a part of the process.

Some effective generic consequences might include the following:

First offense	Reminder
Second offense	Second reminder
Third offense	Conference with student
Fourth offense	Social contract with student
Fifth offense	Conference with parent and administrators

Other consequences should be specifically related to the rule.

If students have some input in the establishment of the consequences, they are more likely to recognize fairness and logic in their implementation. Furthermore, students who accept their consequences, realizing they have not fulfilled their responsibility or obligation, are likely to learn from their mistakes.

THE TEACHER'S ROLE IN SETTING THE CLIMATE

The goal of all teachers is to provide powerful and stimulating lessons so that the students become so "hooked" on the lesson and the group interaction that they have no time to misbehave. The reality, of course, is that no matter how dynamic the teacher and the lesson are, there will always be the student who will try to torpedo any activity by making a "big splash" in the class, creating a whirlpool effect to "pull down" the other students. The teacher's job is to make sure that "big splash" only causes a ripple effect. A few students may succumb to the pull of the disruptive kid, but the rest will manage to "stay afloat" because of the teacher's ability to create his or her own whirlpool of interest, motivation, and respect.

Oftentimes, teachers get angry at the student who is trying to "win over" the class, and they zero in on the ring leader and confront him or her in front of the whole class to show who's the boss. Publicly embarrassing or humiliating students will not make students learn from their mistakes; it will, however, make them try harder not to get caught and it will often make them resentful. As Glasser (1986) states, "For thousands of years we have wrongly concluded that what we do *to* or *for* people can make them behave they way we want even if it does not satisfy them" (p. 20).

Dealing with disruptive students in private, in a fair and consistent manner, and in a manner that maintains their dignity and self-esteem will help them develop an "internal locus of control" and responsibility. Students with an internal locus of control feel guilty when they misbehave, learn from their mistakes, are able to accept the consequences for their actions, and know they can control their actions.

Dealing with disruptive students in front of their peers in an emotional outburst of frustration and anger, however, will lower their self-concept, decrease their desire to cooperate and succeed, and prevent them from developing their own sense of responsibility. They will learn how to become defensive and use an "external locus of control" to blame others for their problems. Consequently, these students rarely accept responsibility for their own actions. Public reprimands, moreover, will eventually destroy the positive climate in any classroom. Students will not feel free to engage in interactive discussions, contribute ideas, or share experiences if they are never sure when they will incur the teacher's wrath or become the object of the teacher's sarcasm or anger. Respecting the dignity of each and every student is essential for effective classroom management.

Teacher Behaviors that Can Erode the Classroom Climate

If students perceive that the teacher is treating them unfairly, they may label that teacher "unfair" or "the enemy." The seeds of insurrection may then be planted, causing a small discipline incident to escalate into a major discipline problem.

Teachers need to be careful in their enforcement of classroom rules and consequences. Sometimes the "message" can be fair, consistent, and positive, but the "delivery system" can be sarcastic, punitive, and negative. Teachers need to model a co-operative value system by treating their own students just like they want their students to treat one another. Some of the essential rules for effective group work can apply to teacher/student interactions.

The following "Dirty Dozen" (see Figure 2) describes the types of teacher behavior that can erode a positive classroom climate and undermine any discipline program—no matter how democratic. Teachers in both subtle and blatant ways can send signals to individual students and to the whole class that jeopardize the caring, cooperative classroom.

Figure 2
Burke's "Dirty Dozen"
Teacher Behaviors that Can Erode the Classroom Climate

1. Sarcasm	Students' feelings can be hurt by sarcastic put-downs thinly disguised as "humor."
2. Negative Tone of Voice	Students can "read between the lines" and sense a sarcastic, negative, or condescending tone of voice.
3. Negative Body Language	Clenched fists, a set jaw, a quizzical look, or standing over a student in a threatening manner can speak more loudly than any words.
4. Inconsistency	Nothing escapes the students' attention. They will be the first to realize the teacher is not enforcing the rules consistently.
5. Favoritism	"Brown-nosing" is an art and any student in any class can point out the "teacher's pet" who gets special treatment. There are no secrets in a class!
6. Put-Downs	Sometimes teachers are not aware they are embarrassing a student with subtle put-downs, but if teachers expect students to encourage rather than put down, they need to model positive behavior.
7. Outbursts	Teachers are sometimes provoked by students and they "lose it." These teacher outbursts set a bad example for the students, create a negative climate, and could lead to more serious problems.

8. Public Reprimands	No one wants to be corrected or humiliated in front of his or her peers. One way to make an enemy out of a student is to make him or her lose face in front of the other students.
9. Unfairness	Taking away promised privileges or rewards; scheduling a surprise test; "nitpicking" while grading homework or tests; or assigning punitive homework could be construed by students as being "unfair."
10. Apathy	Students want teachers to listen to them, show them they are important, and empathize with them. If teachers convey the attitude that teaching is just a job and students are just aggravations that must be dealt with, students will respond accordingly.
11. Inflexibility	Some students may need extra help or special treatment in order to succeed. A teacher should be flexible enough to "bend the rules" or adjust the standards to meet students' individual needs.
12. Lack of Humor	Teachers who cannot laugh at themselves usually have problems motivating students to learn, and usually have boring classes.

Proactive Teachers

The effective classroom teacher anticipates the types of problems that could occur in the classroom and develops a repertoire of strategies to solve the problems. The type of *proactive* approach to preventing discipline problems *before* they occur is far less time-consuming than the *reactive* approach where teachers expend all their energy trying to solve problems *after* they occur. The following procedures could be utilized by the proactive teacher.

Proactive Approaches to Teaching
1. Anticipate potential behavior problems.
   - Don't allow potential problem students to sit together or work together in groups.
   - Seat problem students close to the teacher.

- Give both verbal and written directions to eliminate confusion and frustration that often lead to behavior problems.
- Structure assignments that are relevant, motivating, and developmentally appropriate.
- Follow Glasser's second principle for Quality Schools (Brantigan & McElliott 1991) where students are only asked to do schoolwork they agree has "quality." Don't coerce students into learning facts that, by themselves, have no use in the outside world. Don't teach or test for nonsense.
- Allow enough time for students to complete assignments.
- Make allowances for students with learning disabilities or physical handicaps so they are not frustrated and overwhelmed.
- Pair the potential problem student with a helpful and nurturing partner.
- Encourage peer tutoring to help weaker students complete their work without becoming frustrated.
- Assign a potentially disruptive student to observe an effective cooperative group.
- Conference with students prone to behavior problems to find out if they have some personal or family problems that might be causing them to be upset or uncooperative.
- Talk with parents to find out about any medical problems the student might have.
- Talk with counselors or support personnel to find out about any previous behavior problems the student might have experienced and get suggestions about how to best meet the individual needs of the students.

2.   Diffuse minor problems before they become major disturbances.
   Proximity
   - Move close to the student when you sense a problem developing.

Student-selected time-out
- Allow the student to select a time-out from the class or the group. Let the student go to a desk or chair in the corner of the room to "collect his or her thoughts" or calm down.

Teacher-selected time-out
- Ask the student to go to the time-out area to complete work when his or her behavior is disrupting the group's activity.

3. Address disruptive behaviors immediately.
   - Ask to speak with the student privately in the hall, after class, or after school.
   - Ask the student to explain what he or she thinks the problem is.
   - Send "I-messages" telling the student how his or her behavior affects you. For example, "I feel upset when I see you arguing with your group members."
   - Try to identify the "real problem."
   - Draw up a social contract with the student to develop guidelines for future behavior.
   - Monitor the student's behavior to give specific feedback.
   - Encourage students when they do well.
   - Renegotiate the social contract as needed.
   - Prepare a case study to document chronic misbehaviors and to get outside help if needed.

Sometimes none of the above actions will work and a teacher will have to explore a wider range of strategies to maintain an interactive classroom, foster student cooperation, and promote lifelong learning. The teacher will then be modeling the same problem-solving strategies he or she hopes the students will learn and use in the classroom, the playground, the home, and the workforce.

Problems that require specific strategies to solve will still occur throughout the year, but, hopefully, those problems will be reduced if teachers spend the first three or four weeks of school "laying the groundrules" for the school year.

REFERENCES

Brantigan, N. S., and K. McElliott. 1991. *Creating a quality-based school: A model for the 21st century.* Paper presented at the National Middle School Association Conference, November 8–11, Louisville, Kentucky.

Curwin, R. L., and A. N. Mendler. 1988. *Discipline with dignity.* Alexandria, Va.: Association for Supervision and Curriculum Development.

Evertson, C., and A. Harris. 1991. *Components of effective classroom management: Materials selected from the NDN-approved classroom organization and management program (COMP).* Nashville, Tenn.: Vanderbilt University.

Glasser, W. 1986. *Control theory in the classroom.* New York: Harper & Row.

———. 1990. *The quality school.* New York: Harper Perennial.

Kohn, A. 1991. Caring kids: The role of the schools. *Phi Delta Kappan,* March, 496–506.

A Primer on Classroom Discipline: Principles Old and New

by Thomas R. McDaniel

F ifty years ago, the topic of classroom control was virtually ignored in teacher education programs. Prospective teachers in those days were merely told to make good lesson plans, to be firm but gentle, and not to smile until Christmas. Not so long ago, the behaviorists came up with some interesting insights into the principles of reinforcement. They told teachers to catch the child being good—and to ignore bad behavior. Then the humanists came along and told us that good discipline is related to self-concept and communication. They reminded us to talk to our students as we would address visitors in our homes. Today we are told to be assertive, to negotiate, to analyze transactions, and to rely on logical consequences, reality therapy, and Teacher Effectiveness Training in our dealings with students. When it comes to disciplinary techniques for the classroom, the contemporary teacher suffers from sensory overload.

> When it comes to disciplinary techniques for the classroom, the contemporary teacher suffers from sensory overload.

Meanwhile, everyone—from burned-out teachers and Gallup Poll respondents to a never-ending stream of commissions and task forces—has been telling teachers that discipline must improve, if U.S. education is ever to rise above mediocrity. At the same time, researchers have been generating volumes of

From *Phi Delta Kappan*, vol. 68, no. 1, pp. 63–67, September 1986. © 1986 by Phi Delta Kappa. Reprinted with permission.

data on effective schools and effective teachers. Their studies indicate that certain teaching techniques lead to better learning *and* better behavior. Teachers must master these techniques, the researchers say, if they hope to have well-managed and effective classrooms.

Although all the attention paid to discipline by theorists, the public, and the research community is a bit confusing, the beleaguered teacher has reason for hope. Ten principles—an eclectic combination of traditional and modern, practical and theoretical, pedagogical and psychological—provide some general guidelines for teachers who wish to modify their own behaviors in ways that will yield effective group management and control.

> An in-charge beginning is not repressive authoritarianism; it is the essential first ingredient in a well-mannered classroom.

1. **The focusing principle.** Widely supported by experienced teachers, this principle says, in effect, "Get everyone's attention before giving instructions or presenting material." Beginning teachers often make the mistake of trying to teach over the chatter of inattentive students. They assume that, if they begin the lesson (and there are *many* beginning points within each lesson), students will notice and quiet down. This approach may work occasionally. What the students really learn, however, is that the teacher is willing to compete with them, to speak loudly enough to be heard over the undercurrent, to tolerate inattention, and to condone chatter during instruction.

The focusing principle reminds teachers that, during group instruction, they must request, demand, expect, and wait for attention before they begin to teach. A teacher can say, "I am ready to begin"; "I am ready to begin, boys in the back"; "I am ready to begin, Lillian, and I am waiting for you." The teacher may need to speak loudly, to flip the light switch, to stand with hand raised, to ring a bell—but he or she should insist on, work for, and secure attention *before* starting to teach. Then the teacher can begin the actual instruction in a calm and quiet voice. An in-charge beginning is not repressive authoritarianism; it is the essential first ingredient in a well-mannered classroom.

2. The principle of direct instruction. The point is to get students on-task quickly and to keep them on-task consistently, so that they stay out of trouble. One of the most effective techniques for accomplishing this goal is to clearly state the assignment, the directions, and the time constraints. A teacher might say, for example: "Your task is here on the board, class. You need to use your textbook and the data-bank forms to collect information. You have only 10 minutes to work, so start right away." Some classes respond well when the teacher sets explicit goals: "We took five minutes yesterday just to distribute the construction paper. Let's see if we can distribute the paper in *three* minutes today." To keep students on-task, the teacher should make certain that the tasks are interesting, relevant, and varied and that students are motivated to engage in them. The next three principles also help to keep students on-task.

3. The monitoring principle. "Monitoring" means keeping a constant check on student performance and behavior. Teachers should make personal contact with each student during a lesson, and they should circulate frequently among their students. When students know that the teacher will evaluate their work and behavior from close range and hold them accountable, they are more likely to stay on-task. Monitoring encourages a teacher to move about the classroom and to engage in brief conferences with individual youngsters. These personal encounters enable the teacher to provide individualized instruction or feedback. The focus may be on the academic task at hand ("Freddy, your triangles look fine, but remember to label your angles") or on a student's behavior ("Mabel, put your comb away and begin your math problems, please"). In either case, such quiet conversations between teacher and student can have a significant positive effect on the classroom atmosphere.

4. The modeling principle. Long before the behavioral psychologists told us that students' behavior could be influenced by "models," good teachers recognized the importance of setting an example for their students. (As the adage goes, "Values are caught, not taught.") Teachers who are courteous, prompt, well-organized, enthusiastic, self-controlled, and patient tend to produce students who exhibit similar characteristics, at least to some degree. With sensitivity and tact, teachers can also employ students as models for the other youngsters to emulate.

One especially important modeling technique that teachers should practice is the use of a soft, low-pitched voice. Students find such a voice restful and calming. "Soft reprimands" are also effective because they are not the norm and because, being private, they tend not to invite loud protests, denials, or retorts. It is especially important for teachers to model quiet voice levels when they are circulating among students and monitoring individual work.

5. The cuing principle. Behavioral psychology has given us new insights into the nature and effectiveness of cues (generally, nonverbal reminders about behavioral expectations) in improving classroom discipline. Of course, good teachers have always known that cues improve discipline. The teacher who raises a hand for silence, flips the light switch to get attention, or points to a group of gigglers and then presses an index finger to the lips is reminding students of certain rules, procedures, or expectations.

Some students seem oblivious to classroom cues. In these instances, teachers should 1) examine the cues they are using, 2) establish stronger and more explicit variations of these cues, 3) teach the cues to the students directly, and 4) pair the use of each new cue with a verbal explanation of the cue. A brief example may clarify this approach for the reader. Mrs. Jones always stands with her hands on her hips when she is waiting for attention. If members of the class fail to attend to her in this pose, she may decide to strengthen the cue by combining it with a movement toward the class and a clearing of the throat. Next, she may explain to the students that these cues are designed to let them know that she is waiting for attention. At the next opportunity, she will use the nonverbal cues while saying, "As you can see, class, I am waiting for your attention."

To keep behavioral expectations flowing from teacher to student, a creative teacher can develop a host of novel cues that employ proximity, facial expressions, gestures, and objects (e.g., bells, lights, "clickers") to supplement verbal cues ("Okay, boys and girls, in 10 seconds you will need your protractors"). I know of one teacher who teaches his students new ways to cue *him*, as well. Instead of asking them to raise their hands when they know the answer to a question, he asks them to put their heads on their desks (when they are restless), or to stand up (when they need to stretch), or to pull on their right ear lobes (when they need to be amused). Such experimentation helps students become more sensitive to nonverbal cues as methods of communication. Effective communication is essential to effective discipline.

> A wise teacher manipulates the classroom environment to improve both learning and behavior.

6. **The principle of environmental control.** There are many things in a student's life that a teacher cannot control, such as handicaps, the child-rearing practices of parents, and even whether or not the child eats breakfast each morning. But a wise teacher manipulates the classroom environment to improve both learning and behavior. A teacher can enrich, impoverish, restrict, enlarge, simplify, or systematize the classroom environment. Let us look more closely at a couple of these alternatives for improving discipline.

Often, classroom management is a problem because the students are bored, apathetic, uninterested, or unmotivated. In such situations, a teacher needs to *enrich* the classroom environment in order to improve students' motivation, attention, and involvement.

A teacher might use learning centers, bulletin boards, music, or audiovisual aids to provide a variety of stimuli. He or she could open lessons with exercises requiring inductive reasoning: "Here is a replica of a kitchen implement used by the ancient Egyptians, class. What might they have used it for? What uses might we have for it today?" Enrichment involves consciously adding to or varying the classroom environment for an educational purpose. Done well, enrichment motivates students— and motivated students engage in learning rather than in misbehavior.

However, classroom management can just as frequently be a problem when students are overstimulated by the classroom environment. Overstimulated students have short attention spans, are easily distracted, and tend to be hyperactive. In such situation, a teacher needs to *impoverish* the classroom environment. If the teacher tries instead to be enthusiastic and to motivate students, the result is often disastrous; much like turning up the flame under a bubbling cauldron, the additional stimuli only raise the kinetic energy level in the classroom. Instead, the teacher should darken the room, install carpets, remove distracting materials and diversions, schedule quiet times, create quiet corners, and use such focused teaching approaches as filmstrips and lessons involving directed study. The teacher should also be a model of controlled activity, concentration, and subdued behavior—especially with regard to voice, dress, and movement.

7. The principle of low-profile intervention. This principle is derived from some of the pioneering research on group management by Jacob Kounin, but it is enjoying renewed attention from contemporary researchers. According to this principle, the teacher should manage student behavior as discreetly, unobtrusively, and smoothly as possible—avoiding direct confrontations and public encounters with disruptive students. Without delivering constant orders and commands (i.e., high-profile interventions), the teacher needs to anticipate behavioral problems and to nip them in the bud. A particularly effective approach during large-group instruction is to drop the name of an inattentive student into the middle of an instructional statement: "We need to remember, Clarence, that Columbus was one of several discoverers of America." A teacher can "drop" the names of several students during a presentation, but the name-dropping should be casual, with no hint of reprisal and no pause for reply.

Another low-profile technique is to move close to students who are starting to wander off-task. The teacher's proximity often curtails misbehavior or inattention. Such "overlapping" of teacher behaviors (e.g., moving to a trouble spot in the classroom while continuing to conduct a lesson) becomes almost automatic with practice and can be enhanced by nonverbal cues, such as touching an inattentive student on the shoulder or quietly opening his or her book to the proper page.

8. The principle of assertive discipline. This principle, made popular by Lee Canter, calls for higher-profile but nonhostile interventions that effectively communicate a teacher's wants and needs for better discipline. Actually, assertive discipline is only a commonsense combination of behavioral psychology (praise) and traditional authoritarianism (limit setting).

A teacher should begin by identifying specific roadblocks to discipline; these are usually consequences of the teacher's low expectations regarding students' behavior. All teachers should proceed from the position that no child has the right to prevent classmates from learning or teachers from teaching. Teachers should also believe that their students are able to behave appropriately.

> **All teachers should proceed from the position that no child has the right to prevent classmates from learning or teachers from teaching.**

An assertive teacher communicates these expectations to students through clearly stated and carefully explained rules. When the rules are broken, the teacher consistently follows through with systematic consequences. Meanwhile, the teacher sets limits verbally through requests, hints, and demands, and he or she uses nonverbal communication (eye contact, proximity, touch, gestures) to communicate exactly what is required of whom. Finally, the teacher engages in "broken record" confrontations—repeating requests for compliance until students recognize that the teacher cannot be diverted or ignored. These techniques, coupled with positive consequences for following rules and heeding the teacher's requests, convince students that the teacher knows what he or she wants and needs by way of student behavior. Students also come to realize that their responses will generate positive or negative consequences for *them.*

9. The I-message principle. Both the assertive discipline of Lee Canter and the humanistic discipline of Haim Ginott and Thomas Gordon rely on clear communication between teacher and students. Both approaches to discipline advocate the use of I-messages by teachers. Because assertive discipline and humanistic discipline operate on entirely different premises, however, the I-message takes two forms.

A teacher practicing assertive discipline and the broken-record technique may communicate a demand, wish, or need in order to refocus a group or an individual student. The teacher prefaces his or her specific request with the words "I want you to . . ." or "I need you to . . ." Such I-message assertions are more effective than "You stop . . ." messages, which focus on confrontations ("you") and on past infractions ("stop"). An as-

Figure 1
A Checklist on Discipline for Classroom Teachers

Analyze your classroom disciplinary practices, and place a check in the appropriate column after each item. Then add your points (allowing four points for each "usually," two points for each "sometimes," and zero points for each "never"). Rate yourself as follows: 90–100 = excellent; 80–90 = good; 70–80 = fair; below 70 = poor.

	Usually	Sometimes	Never
1. I get students' attention before giving instruction(s).	☐	☐	☐
2. I wait for students to attend rather than talk over chatter.	☐	☐	☐
3. I quickly get students on-task.	☐	☐	☐
4. I give clear and specific directions.	☐	☐	☐
5. I set explicit time limits for task completion.	☐	☐	☐
6. I circulate among students at work.	☐	☐	☐
7. I hold private conferences/conversations during class.	☐	☐	☐
8. I model courtesy and politeness.	☐	☐	☐
9. I use a quiet voice in the classroom.	☐	☐	☐
10. I use the "soft reprimand" rather than raise my voice.	☐	☐	☐
11. I use a variety of cues to remind students of expected behavior.	☐	☐	☐
12. I teach students my cues.	☐	☐	☐
13. I enrich my classroom to improve students' motivation.	☐	☐	☐
14. I impoverish my classroom to improve attention.	☐	☐	☐
15. I am aware of the effects of my dress, voice, and and movements on student behavior.	☐	☐	☐
16. I use students' names as low-profile correctors of inattention.	☐	☐	☐
17. I use proximity to improve classroom control.	☐	☐	☐
18. I communicate positive expectations of good behavior to my class.	☐	☐	☐
19. I have clear and specific rules that I teach my students.	☐	☐	☐
20. I refuse to threaten or plead with students.	☐	☐	☐
21. I consistently follow through with consequences to enforce rules.	☐	☐	☐
22. I use I-messages assertively to tell students what I want them to do.	☐	☐	☐
23. I use I-messages humanistically to communicate my feelings.	☐	☐	☐
24. I respond to behaviors I like with specific, personal praise.	☐	☐	☐
25. I use nonverbal, social, and activity reinforcers.	☐	☐	☐

sertive I-message tells students exactly what the teacher wants and expects them to *do*.

A teacher practicing humanistic discipline, by contrast, uses I-messages to communicate his or her *feelings,* so that students can understand more clearly how their behavior affects the teacher. According to Gordon, an I-message has three elements: 1) the description of students' behavior ("When you leave our classroom in a mess . . ."); 2) the effect of that behavior on the teacher ("I have to use instructional time for cleaning up . . ."); and 3) the feeling this creates in the teacher ("which frustrates me"). Such messages encourage students to change their behavior voluntarily. Both forms of the I-message have their proper places in the repertoire of the effective classroom manager.

> Punishment does not change students' behavior (except temporarily), but it can increase the incidence of negative behaviors by calling attention to them.

10. The principle of positive reinforcement. One of the best-known methods of classroom management derived from the work of the behaviorists is the "catch 'em being good" principle of positive reinforcement. Punishment does not change students' behavior (except temporarily), but it can increase the incidence of negative behaviors by calling attention to them. A teacher would do better to ignore minor misbehavior, while identifying and praising good behavior. In practice, however, this is easier said than done. Teachers understand the principle of positive reinforcement, but they are not very skillful in applying it. The techniques that follow may help.

One practice that a teacher can employ is to establish *positive* rules and expectations. Once students know that the rule is "Raise your hand for permission to talk," rather than "Do not call out if you have not been recognized," the teacher can praise students for doing the right thing instead of punishing students for doing the wrong thing: "Thank you for raising your hand, George; you have certainly followed our rule to the letter."

Praise is a major technique of positive reinforcement, but it should be sincere, personalized, descriptive, and focused on students' *actions,* not on their characters or personalities. Teachers can set up a positive expectation (e.g., "Let's see how quickly we can distribute the art supplies") and then follow with praise directed at individuals or groups who conform to the expectation (e.g., "The group in the back has set up all the paints and is ready to begin"). A teacher has to *look* for good behavior and then practice describing it in a complimentary fashion.

A teacher can reward good behavior with nonverbal reinforcers (nods, smiles, pats on the back); activity reinforcers (games, field trips, free time); and concrete or token reinforcers (food, stickers, check marks). For example, a teacher might write on the chalkboard each afternoon the names of "super citizens"—students who have made some special contribution that day to the welfare of the class. These students could be the first to go to lunch on the following day. When a class is restless, the teacher might set a timer for a short interval (one to three minutes) and direct students to work quietly until the timer goes off. If they are quiet when the timer goes off (catching them being good), the students should receive a reward— perhaps some free time at the end of the period. Initially, the teacher should set the timer for a short interval, so that the class is almost bound to be on-task when the timer goes off. As the students' study habits and concentration improve, the time should be lengthened. The length of time should not be predictable, however.

Establishing good discipline involves much more than most teachers realize. The 10 principles I have presented here, and the "tricks of the trade" that they generate, are but one aspect of the art of classroom control. In the final analysis, teachers must deal with such dysfunctional behavioral manifestations as hostility, frustration, discouragement, and apathy. Ultimately, then, the quality of a teacher's discipline rests on the quality of his or her instructional practices and long-term relationships with children and on his or her ability to convince young people that school is important. School becomes important to children when teachers reach them with meaningful lessons and a professional attitude that says, "I care about you; I know that you can behave; I want to help you to be a *better* you."

The Vital Link Between Climate, Curriculum, and Assessment

The happy truth is that students learn the curriculum best when we give them power over how they learn it.—Carolyn Mamchur

Establishing a positive climate lays the foundation for a caring, cooperative classroom, but it certainly will not sustain it for more than a few weeks if students are continually subjected to drills on meaningless facts, endless ditto sheets, questions at the end of the chapter, unimaginative lessons, and teacher lectures that provide few opportunities for students to process information and construct meaning for themselves. All the procedures, rules, and consequences in the world will not prevent behavior problems—even by the most highly motivated students.

Glasser feels that until teachers change their curriculum and make learning more meaningful, they will never be able to rid their classrooms of the coercion that causes too many of their students to be their adversaries. Many students, especially at the middle school and high school levels, think the present academic curriculum is not worth the effort it takes to learn it. Additionally, many students resent the tests that require them to memorize "throwaway" information rather than apply what they have learned to real-life situations.

The battle cries to "cover the curriculum," "prepare them for the state tests," and "get them ready for the S.A.T." send the message that knowledge is more important than understanding. However, when students care about what they are studying, have some choices in how they achieve their goals, are allowed to interact with others, and are evaluated authentically by a variety of assessment tools, they understand important concepts and become more prosocial, thereby improving the learning climate of the classroom.

Vito Perrone (1994, *Educational Leadership* 51[5]: 11–12) conducted research for Harvard's Teaching for Understanding project where he asked students when they were most engaged intellectually in the classroom. The following are the common elements they listed:

• Students helped define the content.

• Students had time to wonder and to find a particular direction that interested them.

• Teachers permitted—even encouraged—different forms of expression and respected students' views.

• Teachers were passionate about their work. The richest activities were those invented by the teacher.

• Students created original and public products; they gained some form of "expertise."

• Students *did* something—participated in a political action, wrote a letter to the editor, worked with the homeless, etc.

• Students sensed that the results of their work were not predetermined or fully predictable.

In addition to allowing students to have some choice in selecting their curriculum, Martha Stone Wiske believes that students need to play a bigger role in the assessment process. Too often, students have no control over how they are graded; therefore, they feel powerless. Wiske and many other educators advocate student involvement in the ongoing assessment process of setting goals and criteria for assignments so students know what is expected of them and feel they have been graded fairly.

Teachers who allow students' input in the creation of classroom rules and consequences, curriculum choices, and clear criteria and options for evaluation usually find that they have more successful classes.

The Quality School Curriculum

by William Glasser

ecently I had a chance to talk to the staff members of a high school who had been hard at work for six months trying to change their school into a Quality School. They believed that they were much less coercive than in the past, but they complained that many of their students were still not working hard and that a few continued to be disruptive. They admitted that things were better but asked me if maybe they should reinject a little coercion back into their classroom management in order to "stimulate" the students to work harder.

I assured them that the answer to their complaints was to use less, not more, coercion. At the same time, I realized that in their teaching they had not yet addressed a vital component of the Quality School, the curriculum. To complete the move from coercive boss-managing to noncoercive lead-managing,[1] they had to change the curriculum they were teaching.

> To complete the move from coercive boss-managing to noncoercive lead-managing, they had to change the curriculum they were teaching.

This was made even clearer to me during the break when I talked to a few teachers individually. They told me that they had already made many of the changes that I suggest below and that they were not having the problems with students that most of the staff members were having. Until almost all the teachers change their curriculum, I strongly believe that they will be un-

From *Phi Delta Kappan,* vol. 73, no. 9, pp. 690–694, May 1992. © 1992 by William Glasser. Reprinted with permission.

able to rid their classrooms of the coercion that causes too many of their students to continue to be their adversaries.

In Chapter 1 of *The Quality School,* I briefly cited the research of Linda McNeil of Rice University to support my claim that boss-management is destructive to the quality of the curriculum.[2] From feedback I have been receiving, it seems that the schools that are trying to become Quality Schools have not paid enough attention to this important point. I am partly at fault. When I wrote *The Quality School,* I did not realize how vital it is for teachers to make sure that they teach quality, and I did not explain sufficiently what this means. To correct this shortcoming, I want to expand on what I wrote in the book, and I strongly encourage staff members of all the schools that seek to move to quality to spend a great deal of time discussing this matter.

> **No matter how well the teachers manage them, if students do not find quality in what they are asked to do in their classes, they will not work hard enough to learn the material.**

We must face the fact that a majority of students, even good ones, believe that much of the present academic curriculum is not worth the effort it takes to learn it. No matter how well the teachers manage them, if students do not find quality in what they are asked to do in their classes, they will not work hard enough to learn the material. The answer is not to try to make them work harder; the answer is to increase the quality of what we ask them to learn.

Faced with students who refuse to make much effort, even teachers who are trying to become lead-managers give a lot of low grades—a practice so traditional that they fail to perceive it as coercive. Then the students deal with their low grades by rebelling and working even less than before. The teachers, in turn, resent this attitude. The believe that, because they are making the effort to be less coercive, the students should be appreciative and work harder. The teachers fail to see that the students are not rebelling against them and their efforts to become lead-managers; they are rebelling against a curriculum that lacks quality. Therefore, if we want to create Quality Schools, we must stop *all* coercion, not just some, and one way to do this is to create a quality curriculum.

Before I describe a quality curriculum, let me use a simple nonschool example to try to explain what it is about the curriculum we have now that lacks quality. Suppose you get a job in a factory making both black shoes and brown shoes. You are well-managed and do quality work. But soon you become aware that all the brown shoes you make are sold for scrap; only the black shoes are going into retail stores. How long would you continue to work hard on the brown shoes? As you slack off, however, you are told that this is not acceptable and that you will lose pay or be fired if you don't buckle down and do just as good a job on the brown as on the black. You are told that what happens to the brown shoes is none of your business. Your job is to work hard. Wouldn't it be almost impossible to do as you are told?

As silly as the preceding example may seem, students in schools, even students in colleges and graduate schools, are asked to learn well enough to remember for important tests innumerable facts that both they and their teachers know are of no use except to pass the tests. I call this throwaway information because, after they do the work to learn it, that is just what students do with it. Dates and places in history, the names of parts of organisms and organs in biology, and formulas in mathematics and science are all examples of throwaway information.

Newspapers sometimes publish accounts of widespread cheating in schools and label it a symptom of the moral disintegration of our society. But what they call "cheating" turns out to be the ways that students have devised to avoid the work of memorizing throwaway knowledge. The honest students who are penalized are not pleased, but many students and faculty members and most of the informed public do not seem unduly upset about the "cheating." They are aware that there is no value to much of what students are asked to remember. I certainly do not condone cheating, but I must stress that, as long as we have a curriculum that holds students responsible for throwaway information, there will be cheating—and few people will care.

Elsewhere I have suggested that this throwaway knowledge could also be called "nonsense."[3] While it is not nonsense to ask students to be aware of formulas, dates, and places and to know how to use them and where to find them if they need them, it becomes nonsense when we ask students to memorize this information and when we lower their grades if they fail to do so. Whether called throwaway knowledge or nonsense, this kind of memorized information can never be a part of the curriculum of a Quality School.

This means that in a Quality School there should never be test questions that call for the mere regurgitation of bare facts, such as those written in a book or stored in the memory of a computer. Students should never be asked to commit this portion of the curriculum to memory. All available information on what is being studied should always be on hand, not only during class but during all tests. No student should ever suffer academically because he or she forgot some fact or formula. The only useful way to test students' knowledge of facts, formulas, and other information is to ask not what the information is, but where, when, why, and how it is of use in the real world.

While a complete definition of quality is elusive, it certainly would include usefulness in the real world. And useful need not be restricted to practical or utilitarian. That which is useful can be aesthetically or spiritually useful or useful in some other way that is meaningful to the student—but it can never be nonsense.

In a Quality School, when questions of where, why, when, and how are asked on a test, they are never part of what is called an "objective" test, such as a multiple-choice, true/false, or short-answer test. For example, if a multiple-choice test is used to ask where, why, when, and how, the student in a Quality School should not be restricted to a list of predetermined choices. There should always be a place for a student to write out a better answer if he or she believes that the available choices are less accurate than another alternative. For example, a multiple-choice test question in history might be: "George Washington is called 'the father of his country' for the following reasons: [four reasons would then be listed]. Which do you think is the best reason?" The student could choose one of the listed answers or write in another and explain why he or she thought it better than those listed.

In a Quality School questions as narrow as the preceding example would be rare, simply because of the constant effort to relate all that is taught to the lives of the students. Therefore, if a question asking where, when, why, and how certain information could be used were asked, it would always be followed by the further question: "How can you use this information in your life, now or in the future?"

However, such a follow-up question would never come out of the blue. The real-world value of the material to be learned would have been emphasized in lectures, in class discussions, in cooperative learning groups, and even in homework assignments that ask students to discuss with parents or other adults how what they learn in school might be useful outside of school. The purpose of such follow-up questions is to stress that the curriculum in a Quality School focuses on useful skills, not on information that has no use in the lives of those who are taught it. I define a *skill* as the ability to use knowledge. If we emphasized such skills in every academic subject, there would be no rebellion on the part of students. Students could earn equal credit on a test for explaining why what was taught was or was not of use to them. This would encourage them to think, not to parrot the ideas of others.

> The curriculum in a Quality School focuses on useful skills, not on information that has no use in the lives of those who are taught it.

Continuing with the George Washington question, if a student in a Quality School said that Washington's refusal to be crowned king makes him a good candidate to be considered father of this republic, a teacher could ask that student how he or she could use this information in life now or later. The student might respond that he or she prefers to live in a republic and would not like to live in a country where a king made all the laws. A student's answer could be more complicated than this brief example, but what the student would have thought over would be how Washington's decision affects his or her life today.

Without memorizing any facts, students taught in this way could learn more history in a few weeks than they now learn in years. More important, they would learn to *like* history. Too many students tell me that they hate history, and I find this to be an educational disaster. I hope that what they are really saying is that they hate the history curriculum, not history.

Another important element in the curriculum of a Quality School is that the students be able to *demonstrate* how what they have learned can be used in their lives now or later. Almost all students would have no difficulty accepting that reading, writing, and arithmetic are useful skills, but in a Quality School they would be asked to demonstrate that they can use them. For example, students would not be asked to learn the multiplication tables as if this knowledge were separate from being able to use the tables in their lives.

To demonstrate the usefulness of knowing how to multiply, students would be given problems to solve and asked to show how multiplication helped in solving them. These problems might require the use of several different mathematical processes, and students could show how each process was used. Students would learn not only how to multiply but also when, where, and why to do so. Once students have demonstrated that they know *how* to multiply, the actual multiplication could be done on a small calculator or by referring to tables.

In a Quality School, once students have mastered a mathematical process they would be encouraged to use a calculator. To do math processes involving large numbers over and over is boring and nonessential. Today, most students spend a lot of time memorizing the times tables. They learn how to multiply but fail to demonstrate when, where, and why to multiply. I will admit that the tables and the calculators do not teach students *how* to multiply, but they are what people in the real world use to find answers—a fact finally recognized by the Educational Testing Service, which now allows the use of calculators on the Scholastic Aptitude Test.

Teachers in a Quality School would teach the "how" by asking students to demonstrate that they can do the calculations without a calculator. Students would be told that, as soon as they can demonstrate this ability by hand, they will be allowed to use a calculator. For most students, knowing that they will never be stuck working one long, boring problem after another would be more than enough incentive to get them to learn to calculate.

In a Quality School there would be a great deal of emphasis on the skill of writing and much less on the skill of reading. The reason for this is that anyone who can write well can read well, but many people who can read well can hardly write at all. From grade 1 on, students would be asked to write: first, words; then, sentences and paragraphs; and finally, articles, stories, and letters. An extremely good project is to have each middle school student write a book or keep a journal. Students who do so will leave middle school with an education—even if that is all that they have done.

> For most students, knowing that they will never be stuck working one long, boring problem after another would be more than enough incentive to get them to learn to calculate.

To write a great deal by hand can be onerous, but using a computer makes the same process highly enjoyable. In a Quality School, all teachers would be encouraged to learn word-processing skills and to teach them to their students. Moreover, these skills should be used in all classes. Computers are more readily available in schools today than would seem to be the case, judging from their actual use. If they are not readily available, funds can be raised to buy the few that would be needed. If students were encouraged to write, we would see fewer students diagnosed as having language learning disabilities.

At Apollo High School,[4] where I consult, the seniors were asked if they would accept writing a good letter on a computer as a necessary requirement for graduation. They agreed, and almost all of them learned to do it. One way they demonstrated that their letters were good was by mailing them and receiving responses. They were thrilled by the answers, which we used as one criterion for satisfying the requirement. Clearly, demonstrating the use of what is learned in a real-life situation is one of the best ways to teach.

While demonstrating is the best way to show that something worthwhile has been learned, it is not always easy or even possible to do so. Thus there must be some tests. But, as I stated above, the tests in a Quality School would always show the acquisition of skills, never the acquisition of facts or information alone. Let me use an example from science to explain what would be considered a good way to test in a Quality School. Science is mostly the discovery of how and why things work. But where and when they work can also be important. Too much science is taught as a simple listing of what works—e.g., these are the parts of a cell. Students all over America are busy memorizing the parts of a cell, usually by copying and then labeling a cell drawn in a textbook. The students are then tested to see if they can do this from memory—a wonderful example of throwaway information, taught by coercion. Teaching and testing in this way is worse than teaching no science at all, because many students learn to hate science as a result. Hating something as valuable as science is worse than simply not knowing it.

The tests in a Quality School would always show the acquisition of skills, never the acquisition of facts or information alone.

The students in a Quality School would be taught some basics about how a cell works, and they would be told that all living organisms are made up of cells. To show them that this is useful knowledge, the teacher might bring up the subject of cancer, explaining how a cancer cell fails to behave as normal cells do and so can kill the host in which it grows. All students know something about cancer, and all would consider this useful knowledge.

The subsequent test in a Quality School might ask students to describe the workings of a cell (or of some part of a cell) with their books open and available. They would then be asked how they could use this information in their lives and would be encouraged to describe the differences between a normal cell and a cancer cell. They would be taught that one way to use this information might be to avoid exposure to too much sunlight because excessive sunlight can turn normal skin cells into cancer cells. For most students this information would be of use because all students have some fear of cancer.

Readers might feel some concern that what I am suggesting would not prepare students for standardized tests that mostly ask for throwaway information, such as the identification of the parts of a cell. My answer is that students would be better prepared—because, by learning to *explain* how and why something works, they are more likely to remember what they have learned. Even if less ground is covered, as is likely to be the case when we move from facts to skills, a little ground covered well is better preparation, even for nonsense tests, than a lot of ground covered poorly.

We should never forget that people, not curriculum, are the desired outcomes of schooling. What we want to develop are students who have the skills to become active contributors to society, who are enthusiastic about what they have learned, and who are aware of how learning can be of use to them in the future. The curriculum changes I have suggested above will certainly produce more students who fit this profile.

Will the students agree that these outcomes are desirable? If we accept control theory, the answer is obvious. When the outcomes the teachers want are in the quality worlds of their students, the students will accept them. In my experience skills will be accepted as quality in almost all cases; facts and information will rarely be accepted.

Assuming that skills are taught, the teacher must still explain clearly what will be asked on tests. Sample questions should be given to the students, and the use of all books, notes, and materials should be permitted. Even if a student copies the workings of a cell from a book at the time of the test, the student will still have to explain how this information can be used in life. If students can answer such questions, they can be said to know the material—whether or not they copied some of it.

Tests—and especially optional retests for students who wish to improve their grades—can be taken at home and can include such items as, "Explain the workings of a cell to an adult at home, write down at least one question that was asked by that person, and explain how you answered it." All the facts would be available in the test; it is the skill to use them that would be tested. The main thing to understand here is that, after a school stops testing for facts and begins to test for skills, it will not be long before it is clear to everyone that skills are the outcomes that have value; facts and information have none.

In most schools, the teacher covers a body of material, and the students must guess what is going to appear on the test. Some teachers even test for material that they have not covered. In a Quality School this would not happen. There would be no limitation on input, and the teacher would not ask students to figure out which parts of this input will be on the test. There would be no hands raised asking the age-old question, Is this going to be on the test?

> In most schools, the teacher covers a body of material, and the students must guess what is going to appear on the test. . . . In a Quality School this would not happen.

Since it is always skills that are tested for in a Quality School, it is very likely that the teacher would make the test available to the students before teaching the unit so that, as they went through the material in class, they would know that these are the skills that need to be learned. Students could also be asked to describe any other skills that they have learned from the study of the material. This is an example of the open-endedness that is always a part of testing and discussion in a Quality School. A number of questions would be implicit in all tests: What can you contribute? What is your opinion? What might I (the teacher) have missed? Can you give a better use or explanation?

Keep in mind that, in a Quality School, students and teachers would evaluate tests. Students who are dissatisfied with either their own or the teacher's evaluation could continue to work on the test and improve. Building on the thinking of W. Edwards Deming, the idea is to constantly improve usable skills. In a Quality School, this opportunity is always open.

As I look over what I have written, I see nothing that requires any teacher to change anything that he or she does. If what I suggest appeals to you, implement it at your own pace. Those of us in the Quality School movement believe in lead-management, so there is no coercion—no pressure on you to hurry. You might wish to begin by discussing any of these ideas with your students. In a Quality School students should be aware of everything that the teachers are trying to do. If it makes sense to them, as I think it will, they will help you to put it into practice.

Author's note: These ideas can be found in William Glasser's book The Quality School: Managing Students Without Coercion.

NOTES

1. For a definition of *boss-management* and *lead-management,* see William Glasser, "The Quality School," *Phi Delta Kappan,* February 1990, p. 428.

2. William Glasser, *The Quality School: Managing Students Without Coercion* (New York: Harper & Row, 1990), Ch. 1.

3. See *Supplementary Information Bulletin No. 5* of the Quality School Training Program. All of these bulletins are available from the Institute for Reality Therapy, 7301 Medical Center Dr., Suite 104, Canoga Park, CA 91307.

4. Apollo High School is a school for students who refuse to work in a regular high school. It enrolls about 240 students (9–12) and is part of the Simi Valley (Calif.) Unified School District.

How Teaching for Understanding Changes the Rules in the Classroom

by Martha Stone Wiske

L eaving a door unlocked is the same as giving everyone a key." So warns a sign posted by the campus police in the building where the Teaching for Understanding Project meets every week. But in a funny way, this sign conveys a central message of our project: "*Do* leave the door unlocked, because that's like giving everyone the key."

Understanding is not a private possession to be protected from theft, but, rather, a capacity developed through the free exchange of ideas. Teaching for understanding requires open, explicit negotiation about what knowledge is, how it is developed and defended, and how knowledge is assessed.

At the Harvard Graduate School of Education, our collaborative research with teachers focused initially on developing a language for formulating this approach to teaching and, subsequently, on integrating these principles into classroom practice. The latter proved to be challenging not only because it requires profound rethinking of curriculum and pedagogy, but also because it violates fundamental norms of schools. In their analysis of the social re-

> **Teaching for understanding requires open, explicit negotiation about what knowledge is, how it is developed and defended, whose knowledge counts, and how knowledge is assessed.**

From *Educational Leadership,* vol. 51, no. 5, pp. 19–21, February 1994. © 1994 by the Association for Supervision and Curriculum Development. Reprinted with permission.

alities of teaching, Lieberman and Miller (1992) cite two cardinal rules: Be practical. Be private. The Teaching for Understanding Project violates norms of privacy—taboos against sharing knowledge, authority, and responsibility.

"What norm of privacy?" you may counter: "Aren't schools dedicated to sharing knowledge?" Yes, but the flow of information is primarily in one direction—as is the authority to make decisions about what is taught and how success is defined.

THE LEARNER AS TEACHER

Within classrooms, students are rarely asked to help set the curricular agenda, formulate assessment criteria, or monitor how well those criteria are met. Yet the Teaching for Understanding frameworks asks students to assume important responsibilities in each of these areas.

> **Within classrooms, students are rarely asked to help set the curricular agenda, formulate assessment criteria, or monitor how well those criteria are met.**

A cornerstone of *generative curriculum,* one of four key facets of the project, is that it connects to students' interests and prior knowledge and is designed to help students identify and develop those connections. One teacher who collaborates on this project teaches 7th grade in a school where the assigned central subject is colonial America. One of her tasks is to devise ways of making this subject generative.

As the year drew to a close, she wanted students to focus on biographies of colonial figures. In preparation, she asked each student to read a biography on anybody—from any time and place. With this experience in mind, the class engaged the question, "What kind of window on history does biography provide?" This discussion—itself a valuable performance of students' understandings about the nature of history and historical inquiry—drew out ideas about point of view, bias, and relationships between individual choices and wider social movements. The students' comments proved helpful in two ways. First, their remarks provided material that the teacher later translated into goals and criteria for their research on colonial figures. Second, the discussion informed the students' responses to the teacher's next question: "How shall we decide who are the five most influential people from the colonial period?"

Out of the classroom debate came the sources, forms, and results of historical influence, as well as competing perspectives on these matters. Ultimately, the discussion determined both the process and the results of students' selection of key figures to study. By explicitly using their ideas to shape curriculum and assessment, this teacher signaled to her students that they were intellectual authorities in the classroom learning community.

Providing *ongoing assessment* of *performances of understanding* also violates basic school norms. An important aspect of ongoing assessment is negotiating criteria early and explicitly with students. *Goals for understanding*—the fourth concept in the framework—are stated up front, and criteria for assessing performances are negotiated explicitly. Then teaching and curriculum are designed to work toward these public and consensual standards.

As one teacher said, "I'm making my expert knowledge explicit and sharing it with my students." She is doing this in a recursive and collaborative way. For example, her students read a definition of an essay and then analyzed an essay by E. B. White. Through class discussions, they developed a list of features that made the essay strong, and then drafted their own essays on an assigned topic, attempting to incorporate these features. After reading the drafts, the teacher developed a more refined list of criteria specifying positive features of the essays the class had produced, as well as common problems to be corrected. This sheet became the basis for peer assessment of the next drafts. By "recycling students' ideas," as she put it, the teacher explicitly derived categories and criteria from examples of student work to model a process of analytic thinking.

SHARING INTELLECTUAL AUTHORITY

Proceeding in this way seems to run counter to common expectations of both teachers and students. Articulating understanding goals and assessment criteria with students up front may be difficult for several reasons. First, teachers may never have made these goals explicit for themselves. Second, they may believe that students aren't able to comprehend their criteria until they have developed deeper understanding through participating in the unit. Or teachers may feel that their criteria ought to evolve in response to student's work. On a deeper level, stating goals and criteria up front challenges the kind of authority that teachers are expected to embody.

Stating goals and criteria up front challenges the kind of authority that teachers are expected to embody.

Even the teacher described above, who is deeply committed to sharing intellectual authority with her students, acknowledges that she has to summon all her intellectual self-confidence to quiet a nagging voice that wonders, "If I divulge all I know, will you still respect me in the morning?" Leaving the door unlocked may feel like giving everyone a key that should perhaps not be distributed.

Students conditioned to being told what to learn and whether they have learned may resist teachers' attempts to involve them in self- and peer-assessment. This particular teacher found that her students wanted to see her comments on their papers and her grade at the bottom. Thinking that they did their best work the first time, they doubted their capacity to identify and execute needed improvements. Some parents also questioned the teacher's delegation of authority to students.

In response, the teacher renegotiated expectations with her students and, using consensual standards, demonstrated how to critique their own and peers' work. She also met with parents to discuss the students' portfolios, which illustrated the evolution of their work through cycles of critique and revision. Sharing authority included explicit acknowledgment with students and parents that such sharing contradicts accustomed roles, and it required sustained scaffolding and encouragement.

Another teacher reported that student involvement in assessment was one of the most difficult aspects of the Teaching for Understanding Project. He had originally planned to include a "paired quiz" in the unit that he taught for understanding, but in the end decided against doing this. Later he acknowledged that collaborating on a quiz just didn't seem right to do: "The kids are so conscious of not cheating that this is a violation of the way we've been teaching all along."

The norm against sharing students' knowledge even extends to collaborative learning. According to this teacher, his students didn't think they were learning during collaborative projects. Instead, they regarded group work as "a time to relax, then Mr. K. will tell us what to think." If sharing knowledge during learning is counterintuitive, sharing knowledge during a test is downright criminal.

Although neither paired quizzes nor collaborative learning is required in the Teaching for Understanding framework, both practices are consistent with an emphasis on students' active engagement in making and critiquing their own classmates' knowledge. At root, such activities violate the paradigm that sanctifies knowledge as something the teacher possesses at the beginning, which students acquire during the course, and then demonstrate as their own private possession on a test. To credit students' knowledge, and their capacity to construct and critique knowledge, is to empower students in a way that violates the unspoken norms of most classrooms. Unless this change in the rules of the game is explicitly named and negotiated, students are quite likely to be confused and resistant.

> Teachers who learn model the development of understanding and create a reciprocal relationship with students that legitimates their own struggles to learn.

THE TEACHER AS LEARNER

In a larger sense, the Teaching for Understanding framework encourages teachers to violate norms of privacy that extend to teachers' interactions with their faculty and administrative colleagues. Many teachers say they rarely visit their colleagues, invite them to observe their own classes, or engage in serious conversations about curriculum and pedagogy. How then are teachers to remain active learners?

The teacher as learner is fundamental to teaching for understanding. Teachers who learn model the development of understanding and create a reciprocal relationship with students that legitimates their own struggles to learn. Teachers who learn demonstrate that intellectual authority is provisional because truth is debatable (Peters 1973).

Teachers engaged in the Teaching for Understanding Project have specifically cited discussions with university partners and their fellow teacher-researchers as an important support in their efforts to teach for understanding. These discussions have sometimes provided helpful suggestions about designing curriculum and activities, but, more important, have presented opportunities for reflection, research, and refinement of understandings. As Stenhouse (1983) has argued, research is a necessary basis for teaching.

LEAVING THE DOOR UNLOCKED

Putting a pedagogy of understanding into practice requires a fundamental renegotiation of intellectual authority. What does it mean to be an intellectual authority? Who qualifies to serve in this role? How is authority shared—all of these issues must be addressed if the principles of this project are to be realized.

This renegotiation is no simple matter, for it violates deep-seated, usually unrecognized assumptions and routines concerning the nature of knowledge and the roles of teachers and students. Unless the assumptions underlying practice are deeply challenged, teachers who attempt a pedagogy of understanding may find themselves trying to graft isolated strategies onto the traditional knowledge-transmission paradigm in ways that seem incongruous, confusing, perhaps duplicitous, and possibly counterproductive.

If schools want to support teaching for understanding, they might post the sign about giving away the key as a positive reminder, not a negative warning. Schools and teachers need to develop ways to identify and support successful attempts at unlocking the doors to understanding, shifting from a perspective of intellectual privacy toward one of shared intellectual empowerment—where everyone holds the keys.

Certainly, teachers must not abandon their authority, which derives legitimately from their knowledge of subject matter and their responsibility for guiding students. But they must encourage students to develop their own ways of exercising authority. In short, teachers must be in authority without being authoritarian (Peters 1966).

Author's note: This paper is based on a presentation to the annual meeting of the American Educational Research Association in Atlanta on April 15, 1993. Lois Hetland's authoritative teaching and insightful reflections provided the foundation for much of this research.

REFERENCES

Lieberman, A., and L. Miller. (1992). *Teachers—Their World and Their Work: Implications for School Improvement.* New York: Teachers College Press.

Peters, R. S. (1966). *Ethics and Education.* London: George Allen & Unwin, Ltd.

Peters, R. S. (1973). *Authority, Responsibility, and Education.* New York: Paul S. Eriksson, Inc.

Stenhouse, L. (1983). *Authority, Education, and Emancipation.* London: Heineman Educational Books.

Managing Violent Behaviors in a Student-Centered Classroom

Without interventions, 40 percent of childhood bullies become adult felons.—Larry Brendtro and Nicholas Long

M any professionals feel that the increase in domestic violence and child abuse causes children to resort to violence in school because they view all adults as threatening. Therefore, as Murdock and Gartin point out, children who live with violence at home often do not develop the cognitive processes to develop a sense of self. Without a sense of self, children feel powerless. In order to achieve a sense of power, they may act out, behave aggressively, or carry weapons. Often they become bullies, using physical or verbal attacks, negative gestures, or peer isolation to flaunt their power. These students need to have a sense of belonging, a sense of control, and, in many cases, a sense of routine in their school lives to compensate for the lack of procedures or "sure things" at home. Smith discusses classroom intervention techniques for "possibly the most underrated problem in our schools"—bullying.

Murdick and Gartin describe the factors that can predict which students may develop violent behaviors. They show how teachers and principals can structure school routines, reduce student "down time," and establish classroom rules and expectations as well as a clear explanation of the consequences for inappropriate behavior.

Besides providing the structure at school that is severely lacking in many homes, educators can eliminate the coercion that feeds rebellion, and work instead to foster prosocial behaviors at school that are severely lacking or nonexistent in the family and community. Instead of school administrators bragging about "zero tolerance" for behavior problems, schools should strive to create a safe, inclusive environment for all students (not just the good students) and to resocialize troublesome students. As Brendtro and Long write, "Excluding violent students from an education is no more moral than forcing the most critical patients from an emergency room. These students need to belong *somewhere.*"

How to Decrease Bullying in Our Schools

by Susan J. Smith

P ossibly the most underrated problem in our schools and and neighborhoods is bullying, and it is a problem that demands immediate attention. Research indicates that one in seven students is either a bully or has been the victim of a bully (Olweus 1987).

Bullying takes four main forms: physical attacks, verbal harassment, negative gestures, and peer isolation. Although boys are most often involved in physical bullying, girls share equally in the other three forms.

Victims of bullying are often either handicapped, overweight, physically small, or display such vulnerable characteristics as anxiety, insecurity, sensitivity, and shyness. They often will go out of their way to avoid "unsafe turf," and can develop stress-related somatic symptoms such as headaches. As a result of bullying, victims may miss a lot of school, become underachievers, display poor self-concepts, run away from home, and even attempt suicide (Greenbaum 1987).

> **Research indicates that one in seven students is either a bully or has been the victim of a bully.**

Bullies, on the other hand, are usually underachievers and are five times more likely than other children as they grow older to be cited in juvenile court, to have more traffic violations, and be more abusive to their spouses and children (Eron 1987).

Bullying in school can be drastically decreased through careful intervention, beginning with student and adult aware-

From *Principal,* vol. 72, no. 1, pp. 31–32, September 1992. © 1992 by the National Association of Elementary School Principals. Reprinted with permission.

ness of the magnitude and depth of the problem. People are not born bullies. It is a learned behavior affected by environmental factors related to the family, peer groups, and mass media. A few of these factors that directly contribute to learned aggressive behavior are:

• Parent overindulgence in permitting children to observe violence on television and in movies

• Inadequate parental monitoring of children's whereabouts and friendships

• Unassertive, inconsistent, and unsupportive home discipline

• Acceptance of aggressive behavior in males as normal and expected (Eron 1987).

Because victims of bullying are often reluctant to report abuse to parents and teachers, it is vital for others to identify and intervene in bullying situations. There is no reason for 2 percent of the student body to have the power to intimidate the other 98 percent, but to change this pattern takes a pledge by everyone—parents, teachers, administrators, and students—to make our schools a safe, secure, and motivating environment.

"NOBODY LIKES A BULLY"

One method being used in some South Carolina elementary schools is an instructional unit and training video called "Nobody Likes a Bully." It is designed to raise the awareness level of students in grades 3 through 6 about bullying and its effects, after which the students are asked to participate in a Student Watch program, where they are taught the peer negotiation skills needed to help themselves and others in conflict situations.

The Student Watch program stresses that students are to handle problems with their heads and hearts, not their hands. Student representatives are trained to encourage their peers to talk about whatever is bothering them and, if possible, to try to work out solutions without adult intervention (Cahoon 1988). What the representatives are trained *not* to do is scold, make demands, pass judgments, or force their services on others.

Teachers in third through sixth grades appoint boy and girl Student Watch representatives each day, rotating the appointments so that every student is involved. The representative serves as a peer model while keeping an eye out for potential bullying situations in the lavatories, playground, cafeteria, and other public areas.

In such cases, it is the representative's job to encourage classmates to calmly communicate to each other what is upsetting them, and give them an opportunity to work out a peaceful solution. If the students agree to a resolution, and shake hands, nothing is reported to the teacher. However, if the problem cannot be solved, or has escalated beyond the point where the representative can help, the teacher is immediately notified.

Included in the "Nobody Likes a Bully" unit are optional pre- and post-program surveys, which can help determine the unit's effectiveness. When the unit was field-tested in four South Carolina elementary schools, the surveys revealed that:

• Of the 2,289 students who answered the pre-program survey, two-thirds—1,518—said they had been bullying victims.

• More than 64 percent thought bullying was a problem in their school, and more than 83 percent said they would like school better if most of the bullying could be stopped.

• Of the 2,086 students who answered the post-program survey, 54 percent said they felt that bullying was now less of a problem, and 66 percent said they liked school better.

• Almost three-quarters of the students said they enjoyed being Student Watch representatives, while only 15 percent considered the position to be "scary."

In addition, the principals of the four schools reported a 50 percent reduction in the number of referrals to their offices after the program had been in effect for only eight weeks.

It is true that when you raise the awareness level of a group of people concerning a problem like bullying, there usually will be a temporary decrease in the problem. However, for there to be a long-range effect, prevention programs like Student Watch must become integral parts of schoolwide discipline efforts and students need to be involved throughout the year. Bullying in our nation's schools is a serious problem that cannot be solved by adults alone.

REFERENCES

Cahoon, P. "Mediator Magic." *Educational Leadership*, January 1988: 92–94.

Collins, G. "Studying the Behavior of Bully and Victim." *New York Times*, May 12, 1986.

Eron, L. D. "Aggression Through the Ages." *School Safety*, Fall 1987: 12–16.

Greenbaum, S. "What Can We Do About Schoolyard Bullying?" *Principal*, November 1987: 21–24.

Kniveton, B. H. "Peer Models and Classroom Violence: An Experimental Study." *Educational Research*, June 1986: 111–115.

Maher, R. "Students Watch Out for Their Own." *School Safety*, Fall 1987: 26–27.

Olweus, D. "Schoolyard Bullying—Grounds for Intervention." *School Safety*, Fall 1987: 4–11.

Perry, D. G. "How Is Aggression Learned?" *School Safety*, Fall 1987: 23–25.

Roberts, M. "Schoolyard Menace." *Psychology Today*, February 1988: 53–56.

Roderick, T. "Johnny Can Learn to Negotiate." *Educational Leadership*, January 1988: 86–90.

Romney, D. *Dealing with Abnormal Behavior in the Classroom*. Bloomington, Ind.: Phi Delta Kappa, 1986.

Sayger, T.; Horne, A.; and Walter, J. "Behavioral Systems Family Counseling: A Treatment Program for Families with Disruptive Children." *Contemporary Education*, Spring 1987: 160–166.

Selman, R. L., and Glidden, M. "Negotiation Strategies for Youth." *School Safety*, Fall 1987: 18–21.

Stephens, R. D. "NSSC Report: Educating the Public about Bullies." *School Safety*, Fall 1987: 2.

How to Handle Students Exhibiting Violent Behaviors

by Nikki L. Murdick and Barbara C. Gartin

T oday's teachers and student are constantly at risk because of the increase in violent crimes within schools. According to the Uniform Crime Report (1981), 18.5 percent of all arrests involving violent crime are committed by individuals who are under the age of eighteen. In fact, it has been estimated that juvenile misconduct of a violent nature leading to adjudication may occur in up to 95 percent of the nation's youth under the age of twenty-one (Siegel and Senna 1981). Often these children and youths are labeled unofficially as delinquent, conduct disordered, or antisocial (Rock 1992). Whatever the label, though, various forms of juvenile misconduct, rule breaking, and especially violent behaviors are commonplace in public schools today.

> **Whatever the label, various forms of juvenile misconduct, rule breaking, and especially violent behaviors are commonplace in public schools today.**

Continued occurrences of violent behaviors instill fear in both the teachers and the students who attend the public schools (Boesel 1978). Needless to say, this atmosphere is not conducive to the provision of a safe environment in which to learn. Because of this fear as well as other contributing factors, many students believe that for their protection they must carry some type of weapon to school (*Parade Magazine* 1992). In this article we will try to alleviate some of these fears by discussing

From *The Clearing House,* vol. 66, no. 5, pp. 278–280, May/June 1993. © 1993 by Heldref Publications. Reprinted with permission of the Helen Dwight Reid Educational Foundation.

possible causes of violence in the classroom and by outlining steps to prevent or reduce the impact of students who exhibit violent behaviors.

CAUSES OF THE INCREASE IN CLASSROOM VIOLENCE

The question most frequently asked is, "What is causing this explosion in the number of violent crimes in the schools?" The cause for the increase in violence within the classroom continues to be researched. Many professionals believe that increase in domestic violence and child abuse results in children who display learning and behavior characteristics that lead to frustration, school failure, and even retaliatory violence. According to Craig (1992), "living with violence inhibits the cognitive processes by which a child develops an awareness of the self." This lack of self-awareness results in a feeling of powerlessness and may lead to the child seeing adults as threatening rather than as supporters and providers of their innate needs. A sense of personal power is perceived as essential to all people, and many children find that bringing weapons to school provides them with that sense of power. Associated with the need for power is the children's need to have a sense of control in their lives. Many children have no feeling of control or sense of routine in their lives. Often this lack of routine and control are a result of abuse or violence occurring within the home or community. Other children lack routine or the feeling of control because of homelessness or poverty. Children in these situations may also lack feelings of significance and competency. When these four needs are unmet, children may turn to violence to fulfill them.

STEPS TO TAKE TO COUNTER VIOLENT BEHAVIORS

Teachers in today's schools must be aware that, no matter the personal characteristics of the teacher or how caring the teacher may be, the occurrence of violent behaviors within the classroom is highly probable. Indeed, these violent behaviors may involve guns, knives, brass knuckles, or other weapons. Therefore, teachers must be proficient in the identification of factors that may be predictive of violence. Teachers must be trained to lessen the possibility of violence through the arrangement of the learning environment. Furthermore, teachers must develop classroom procedures to provide for their safety and the safety of their students if violence should occur within the classroom. Without this preparation, the teachers will place themselves in a reactive position, which may result in interventions that may escalate the student's violent outburst (Epanchin 1991).

Identification of Factors Predictive of Violence

Predictors of possible violent behaviors by a student include (a) evidence of past or continuing participation in violent behavior (Keilitz and Dunivant 1987; Monahan 1982); (b) evidence of the child's being a victim of abuse (Craig 1992); (c) evidence of a family climate of violence including verbal threats (Patterson, Reid, Jones, and Conger 1975; Patterson 1982); (d) evidence of the student's exhibiting cruelty to animals (Sinclair and Alexson 1992); (e) presence of a subculture supporting aggression as a positive attribute (Bandura 1976); and (f) a history of temper tantrums and verbal aggression (Schloss and Smith 1987). Other factors that are believed to be indicative of possible violence include (a) involvement in a timeout situation (Rosenberg, Wilson, Maheady, and Sindelar 1992); (b) the release from incarceration; (c) the cessation of medication for violent or self-injurious behaviors; (d) the presence in the classroom of a student who is often victimized (Epanchin 1991); (e) the availability of a weapon.

> Teachers must be trained to lessen the possibility of violence through the arrangement of the learning environment.

Arrangement of the Learning Environment

Prior to the beginning of the school year, a thorough review of the school environment should be conducted to identify potentially dangerous sites. These sites include possible hiding places, unsupervised restroom areas, stairwells, window or doorway glass that may be not be shatterproof, and school equipment that might be used as weapons. When dangerous sites cannot be appropriately corrected, then school personnel should be assigned to supervise these areas.

The instructional environment should then be evaluated for factors that may encourage violent behavior. Instruction should be planned to eliminate or effectively reduce the student down-time (Kounin 1970). Classroom rules and expectations should be clearly explained and a reinforcement program for appropriate behaviors should be initiated (Jones and Jones 1990). The teacher should also provide a clear explanation of the consequences of inappropriate behaviors (Anderson, Evertson, and Emmer 1980; Emmer, Evertson, and Anderson 1980). Teachers should guard against the use of punitive, confrontational, and deprecatory methods because these have been shown to increase the possibility of violent reactions from students (Rock 1992). Students who exhibit violent behavior often do not employ appropriate methods of communicating feelings of anger and use a verbal style that lacks verbal mediation skills (Camp 1977). Instruction in appropriate communication methods in stressful situations should be an essential part of the educational program throughout the school year.

Instruction in appropriate communication methods in stressful situations should be an essential part of the educational program throughout the school year.

The establishment of rapport with the children is essential for effective instruction. Additionally, a routine must be established in the classroom (Epanchin 1991). This routine must begin with the arrival of the first student and continue until the departure of the last student. Presentation of the lessons should also follow predetermined procedures to eliminate the unexpected from the instructional time (Rosenshine and Stevens 1986). If the instructional situation results in surprising or spontaneous events in which the student perceives danger or loss of power, violent behaviors may occur (Craig 1992). The teacher must remember that whenever the child perceives danger, any person may be viewed as a threat, even a person who usually is considered a "friend," with violent behaviors being the possible result (Craig 1992).

Emergency Procedures and Drills

Before school begins each year, teachers should develop classroom procedures concerning violent behavior and provide opportunities for the practice of these procedures in case violence does occur. These procedures must be complementary with the school's policies on discipline so that support from the school administration concerning the procedures being developed can be obtained. After the policies have been developed, any personnel who will be responsible for assisting in the practice and usage of such policies must be trained to carry them out without question should the need occur.

Procedures to use when students become violent and/or have a weapon should be taught during the first weeks of class. Students should be taught to respond to the statement "Drill" by walking quietly behind the teacher and out of the classroom. Students should be reminded not to walk behind or near the child who is violent. One student should be identified as having the responsibility of contacting the school office, which will notify the authorities of the incident occurring in the classroom.

Procedures to use when students become violent and/or have a weapon should be taught during the first weeks of class.

If a student threatens violence or produces a weapon, the teacher should assess the situation to ascertain what actions should be taken. The teachers should look for any physical or behavioral evidence of drug usage as the use of drugs may prohibit the student from responding to the teacher in a reasonable manner. The teacher should also determine if the classroom should be evacuated at the time of the incident or at the earliest opportunity. The classroom should be evacuated by using the previously established and practiced procedures. The attention of the person threatening violence should be focused on the teacher. This can be accomplished by the teacher taking two steps back and then sitting down or standing behind furniture that can be overturned for the teacher's protection. After the teacher is behind the desk or table, both hands should be placed flat on the table in view, but with thumbs under the edge. This will enable the teacher to overturn the furniture, crouching behind it, and using it as a shield for protection if such action is needed.

The teacher should encourage the child exhibiting the violent behavior to leave the room by using non-threatening statements such as "You might want to take a break now." The teacher should always face the child and not block the door. If the child will not leave the classroom, the teacher should say to the child in a gentle tone of voice, "Please put down the (weapon) so we can talk." The teacher should ask, "Are you angry with me?" Remember attempts to establish control through the use of an authoritative voice or imperative statements, such as "Give me that (weapon)," should be avoided. It is important that at all times the student be treated with respect. Eye contact should be maintained, but not as an instrument in a contest of wills. Verbal statements should be used that are non-threatening and should be spoken in a tone of voice that is firm, yet gentle. The teacher should never attempt to humiliate or frighten the student as this will usually escalate the situation. The child should be given choices, not orders.

Body language that is non-threatening should always be used. For example, the teacher should stand with an open stance, keeping hands at the side of the body in view of the child and not behind the back or on the hip. Pointing is viewed by most students as a threatening move.

CONCLUSION

Violent behavior is an increasing problem in our society today. One teacher is quoted as saying about the first day of school with students exhibiting violent behaviors that

> . . . my teacher training hadn't prepared me for aggressive student behavior. I learned children can be much more violent than I'd ever expected, and I found that the activities I planned actually contributed to my students' aggressive behaviors. I had to learn how to control the class soon or someone would be badly injured (Rosenberg et al. 1992, 233).

But those teachers who are aware of factors related to classroom violence, who have developed instructional strategies to prevent violence from occurring, and who have implemented procedures for resolving the potential crisis should one occur are better prepared to handle these situations in a safe manner.

REFERENCES

Anderson, L., C. Evertson, and E. Emmer. 1980. Dimensions in classroom management derived from recent research. *Journal of Curriculum Studies* 12: 343–56.

Bandura, A. 1976. Social learning analysis of aggression. In *Analysis of delinquency and aggression*, edited by E. Ribes-Inesta and A. Bandura. Hillsdale, N.J.: Erlbaum.

Boesel, D. 1978. *Violent schools—safe schools: The safe school study report to the Congress.* Vol. 1. Washington, D.C.: National Institute of Education.

Camp, B. 1977. Verbal mediation in young aggressive boys. *Journal of Abnormal Psychology* 86:145–53.

Craig, S. E. 1992. The educational needs of children living with violence. *Phi Delta Kappan* 74(1):67–71.

Emmer, E., C. Evertson, and L. Anderson. 1980. Effective management at the beginning of the school year. *Elementary School Journal* 80: 219–31.

Epanchin, B. C. 1991. Discipline and behavior management. In *Educating emotionally disturbed children and youth: Theories and practices for teachers*, 2nd ed., edited by J. L. Paul and B. C. Epanchin, 374–412. New York: Merrill.

Jones, V., and L. Jones. 1990. *Comprehensive classroom management.* Boston: Allyn and Bacon.

Keilitz, I., and N. Dunivant. 1987. The learning disabled offender. In *Special education in the criminal justice system*, edited by C. M. Nelson, R. B. Rutherford, and B. I. Wolford. Columbus, Ohio: Merrill.

Kounin, J. 1970. *Discipline and group management in classrooms.* New York: Holt, Rinehart, and Winston.

Monahan, J. 1982. Childhood predictors of adult criminal behavior. In *Early childhood intervention and juvenile delinquency*, edited by F. N. Dutile, C. H. Foust, and D. R. Webster, 11–21. Lexington, Mass.: Heath.

Parade Magazine. 1992. Parade's special intelligence report: Drug drills. (26 Sept.): 26.

Patterson, G. R. 1982. *Coercive family processes.* Eugene, Oregon: Castalia Press.

Patterson, G., J. Reid, R. Jones, and R. Conger. 1975. *Families with aggressive children.* Eugene, Oregon: Castalia Press.

Rock, E. E. 1992. High-incidence behavior disorders. In *Educating students with behavior disorders*, edited by M. S. Rosenberg, R. Wilson, L. Maheady, and P. T. Sindelar, 35–85. Boston: Allyn and Bacon.

Rosenberg, M. S., R. Wilson, L. Maheady, and P. T Sindelar. 1992. *Educating students with behavior disorders.* Boston: Allyn and Bacon.

Rosenshine, B., and R. Stevens. 1986. Teaching functions. In *Handbook of research on teaching,* 3rd ed., edited by M. C. Wittrock, 376–91. New York: Macmillan.

Schloss, P., and M. Smith. 1987. Guidelines for the use of manual restraint in public school settings for behaviorally disordered students. *Behavioral Disorders* 12:1–14.

Siegel, L. J., and J. J. Senna. 1981. *Juvenile delinquency: Theory, practice, and law.* New York: West.

Sinclair, E., and J. Alexson. 1992. Relationship of behavioral characteristics to educational needs. *Behavioral Disorders* 17(4): 292–304.

Uniform Crime Report. 1981. *Crime in the United States.* Washington, D.C.: U.S. Government Printing Office.

Watanabe, A. 1992. Managing rule breaking and delinquency. In *Educating students with behavior disorders,* edited by M. S. Rosenberg, R. Wilson, L. Maheady, and P. T. Sindelar, 297–334. Boston: Allyn and Bacon.

Breaking the Cycle of Conflict

by Larry Brendtro and Nicholas Long

Land where the bullets fly—
Land where my brothers die—
From every street and countryside,
Let us run and hide.

An urban youngster sings this corrupted version of the patriotic "My Country 'Tis of Thee." His feelings of fear and helplessness are shared by thousands of young people. Living in environments of violence, they learn to watch their backs, not look to their futures. These are the psychological orphans, children of rage and rebellion who are forever biting the hand that didn't feed them.

Considering the scale of violence in our culture, it is surprising that citizens are so ill-informed about its causes and cures. Perhaps this is because those who shout the loudest know the least, particularly politicians who exploit the public fear of crime. Trapped in survival-mode mentality, the public wastes resources fighting delinquents instead of delinquency.

Violence is particularly threatening when it invades our schools. Since passage of the inclusive provision in the Education for All Handicapped Children Act (P.L. 94-142) in 1975, schools have had a *zero reject* legal obligation to educate all children, including those with emotional and behavioral handicaps. Many schools strive to create safe, inclusive environments for all students and to resocialize troublesome students. Other edu-

From *Educational Leadership*, vol. 52, no. 5, pp. 52–56, February 1995. © 1995 by the Association for Supervision and Curriculum Development. Reprinted with permission.

cators, driven by the catch phrase *zero tolerance,* resort to punishment and expulsion. They are assisted in this not-in-my-backyard mentality by a cottage industry of legal consultants (Walker 1993).

True, there must be consequences for school violence. School officials need the power to make provisions for students who endanger others; all students—offenders and victims alike—need the security of a school safe from violence. But, as Goodlad (1993) posits, if we cease trying to teach difficult students, we shift the responsibility for their enculturation elsewhere—and there is no elsewhere. Excluding violent students from an education is no more moral than forcing the most critical patients from an emergency room. These students need to belong *somewhere.*

> If we cease trying to teach difficult students, we shift the responsibility for their enculturation elsewhere—and there is no elsewhere.

Like the common cold, violence is hard to explain or eradicate. More than three decades ago, the two of us began our work with "children who hate," as they then were called by our teachers, Fritz Redl and David Wineman (1957). The ensuing years have brought us into direct contact with thousands of such youths. Careers in "aggression immersion" discourage many dedicated people. At times one wants to surrender and retreat into a private cocoon. Eleanor Guetzloe, our colleague and author of dozens of publications on youth suicide, recently shifted her research focus to youth violence. She was promptly amazed at how complex this problem is compared to the more manageable task of understanding youth suicide.

ROOTS OF VIOLENCE

Violence is behavior that *violates* another individual. An umbrella term, it describes a variety of destructive personality traits and antisocial behaviors. It is present in all societies, but the level of violence varies greatly among cultures. Extreme, chronic violence is a sure sign that something is awry in the child or the community. Similarly, aggression is programmed into the biological beast in all of us; in threatening situations, inborn protective mechanisms tell us to fight or flee. Violent aggression, however, is not endemic to the human experience.

Violence is a highly moralistic concept; it tends to evoke highly charged debate. The National Council on Crime and Delinquency has proposed replacing the rhetoric of moral condemnation with a preventive public health approach. While still holding youth accountable for their behavior, this orientation would clarify the origins of violence and the avenues for rational intervention (Krisberg and Austin 1993).

> Today, the orphanages are gone, but we are mass-producing hordes of adult-detached children.

In this spirit, we have identified four protective factors that eliminate or curb violence: social bonds, stress and conflict resolution, cultural sanctions, and brain controls. In the absence of these factors, violence is unleashed.

1. Broken Social Bonds

The most powerful restraints on violent behavior are healthy human attachments. These originate in early relationships of parental affection and guidance. Securely attached, children learn trust, competence, self-management, and prosocial behavior. Early in this century, psychiatrists, including David Levy and Lauretta Bender, found that children reared in depersonalized orphanages developed "affect hunger" or "affectionless personality" (Karen 1994). When the social bond between child and adult was not nurtured, conscience was impaired and children did not internalize values. These unbonded children were labeled antisocial, primitive-unsocialized, or sociopathic.

Today, the orphanages are gone, but we are mass-producing hordes of adult-detached children. More families are disrupted by divorce, abuse, poverty, drugs, and other forces that interfere with normal parenting. Adults who own lives are chaotic cannot effectively monitor and manage children's activities or affiliations. Nor can they spend time with children, teach conflict-resolution skills, or communicate consistent behavioral expectations (Walker 1993).

Historically, extended families or tribes provided social bonds. Theologian Martin Marty observes that even though parents often were too young and immature, or may have died early, the tribe carried on cultural values. Today, having lost our tribes, we rely on a tiny nuclear family of one or two over-stressed parents. Schools are now being asked to become new tribes, but seldom are prepared to play this role. When families fail, however, the only alternative institution for re-education is prison.

Angry adult-wary youths do not fare well in factory schools. They gravitate to other alienated people—gangs and other negative peer subcultures, or predatory adults like pimps, pedophiles, or criminal mentors. In these "artificial belong-ings," they acquire training and support for antisocial lifestyles. Relishing freedom from adult authority, they never gain true in-dependence because they have not known secure dependence. "Nobody tells me what to do!" they shout, masking the reality that nobody really cares. Since they do not care either, their vio-lence can be calculated and cold-blooded, motivated by money, power, status, revenge, racism, and hedonistic pleasure and aggression.

Although understanding teachers could offer surrogate bonds, these children's behavior drives most adults away. More-over, school discipline rooted in punishment or exclusion only further estranges these students. Even specialized alternative programs seldom provide little more than what Knitzer and colleagues call "a curriculum of control" (1990).

2. Stress and Conflict
In manageable doses, stress is a normal product of living. Most children handle it reasonably well; they are resilient and thrive in spite of challenges. But others are overwhelmed and behave in self-destructive or antisocial ways.

Sources of stress abound: normal adolescent development, family conflict, poverty, the mean streets of dangerous neigh-borhoods. When stress is severe and prolonged, children adopt ingrained styles of defensive behavior. They may have a hostile bias toward all adults, carry a menacing interpersonal demeanor to school, and believe that respect can be gained only through intimidation.

Schools themselves are major stressors for many students. Daily, students risk bad grades, bullies, and peer rejection. Sociologists have identified patterns of "school-induced delinquency" caused by school failure (Gold and Osgood 1993). Unable to secure self-esteem in positive ways, some students seek status through antisocial behavior.

> Unable to secure self-esteem in positive ways, some students seek status through antisocial behavior.

Students may harbor dark conflicts that explode in school. We recall an 8th grade boy who, for no apparent reason, battled peers and teachers for a year. Finally, the boy revealed that he was being sexually abused and threatened by an adult neighbor. If nobody had helped, stress could have become unbearable, possibly resulting in extreme violence to himself or others. Mones (1993) has worked with hundreds of severely abused children who developed post-traumatic stress disorders. Overwhelmed with fear and rage, they killed their tormentors.

Schools traditionally approach behavioral crises by demanding compliance with rules. Sometimes this works, but troubled behavior may mask problems that adults need to understand. For example:

> A newly enrolled 3rd grader became wild and disrespectful, resulting in almost daily removal from class. It was several weeks before the staff discovered that he and his siblings had been abandoned by their mother shortly after they moved to a deserted farm. Fearful of being separated, the children told no one and continued riding the bus to school each day.

Many children carry to school each morning a stack of accumulated stressors from the night before. For them, schools need to be a refuge where their lives can be put back in balance (Garbarino 1992). Those who simply punish are often the last to discover what is causing a child's life to fall apart.

A "conflict cycle model" that Long (1990) has developed can teach professionals, parents, and students how to keep stressful situations from escalating. An aggressive student under stress creates these same feelings in peers or adults. People who are not trained to recognize these feelings will act on them and mirror or duplicate the aggressive student's behavior. For example, a youth shouts at a peer to "fuck off," and the normal impulse is to retort "*you* fuck off." Thus the conflict cycle whirls into retaliation. Long's analysis of hundreds of crisis incidents shows that most originate from problems outside of school, but escalate to violence because participants cannot disengage from confrontations.

3. A Culture of Violence

Societies placing clear, consistent, reasonable sanctions on acts of aggression do not mass-produce violent children. The United States has strong laws against violence, but they are inconsistently applied and compete with pervasive proviolence messages. Most violence is a private affair, in abusive homes ruled by petty tyrants. But America's infatuation with violence extends to the media, sports, politics, the military, and even church and school. From the O.J. Simpson trial to abortion protests to brutal rap music and talk show themes, there is no avoiding it. Even cartoons are violent, and it has been shown that children who watch them consistently are more aggressive than their peers.

We educators have a responsibility to try to stress-proof students against this onslaught. By analyzing violence in the media and the meaning of the sportsmanship, we may help inoculate children from these proviolence messages. Rather than moralizing, we should ask questions like, "Do you think this film would be damaging to your younger brothers and sisters?" The maturity that young people show in such discussions can be heartening.

4. Unhealthy Brains

With so much learned violence, educators often overlook neurologically triggered aggression. Only an intact, rational, sober brain can control angry impulses. Violence, however, is frequently a by-product of intoxication. Mental illnesses due to neurological trauma, disease, or chemical imbalances can also cause impaired thinking and perception.

Research on young people awaiting execution for murders offers dramatic evidence of how such abnormalities foster violence: half of the youths on death row have histories of brain trauma or dysfunction.

Alcohol and other drug abuse chemically alters brain states, leading to loss of self-control, angry outbursts, and deadly violent acts. In the view of pollster George Gallup Jr., America does not have a crime problem: it has an alcohol and drug problem. A recent report to Congress tied alcohol to 49 percent of murders and 52 percent of rapes. By 9th grade, 90 percent of young people have tried alcohol and a third of 12th graders are binge drinkers. Of particular concern is the impact of chemicals on fetal brains. Babies with fetal alcohol syndrome and crack babies are at risk for later violence because brain damage can impair cognitive controls and social bonding.

Psychiatrist Robert Hunt (1993) has summarized research on the neurobiological roots of aggression. He observed that in some children with prefontal-cortical deficits, the slightest irritation can trigger rage. People with paranoid disorders may plot revenge, setting off a predatory pattern of brain activation like that of a stalking lion. Extremely hyperactive children manifest tornado-like aggression, which passes as quickly as it begins. Hunt speculates that even psychologically based aggression can cause secondary impairment in brain functioning.

When educators suspect organic problems, their responsibility is primarily to secure appropriate diagnosis and treatment. However, in the battle against substance abuse, schools are major players. A wide range of curriculums and student service programs are available to combat substance abuse (Brendtro et al. 1993). It is crucial to teach about the fetal damage chemicals cause, and to support teenage mothers and fathers so they will succeed in the dual roles of student and parent.

VICTORIES IN VIOLENCE PREVENTION

One can easily rationalize that only total social reform will reduce violence. But educators can achieve major victories by concentrating on one child, one classroom, and one school at a time. While refusing to oversimplify violence or be overwhelmed by it, we must fight this war on three fronts:

1. Primary Prevention

This should be our highest priority, particularly for young children. Troubled behavior is self-perpetuating. We must:

   • Prevent "broken belongings." We inoculate children against violence by meeting their most basic need—a consistent, safe, loving environment. We must redesign schools to restore the sense of tribe, and our communities must develop comprehensive early childhood and family support centers. Some middle schools and small alternative high schools also have created secure home-like living arrangements for students.

> We inoculate children against violence by meeting their most basic need—a consistent, safe, loving environment.

   • Teach self-discipline. Beginning in elementary school, we must give all children basic training in discipline, but not the boot-camp variety. Charney (1993) proposes a curriculum for "ethical literacy," where teachers use naturally occurring discipline problems to teach self-discipline and create cultures of nonviolence.

   • Teach conflict resolution. The "peacemakers" curriculum (Johnson and Johnson 1991) teaches children to handle conflicts and rule violations through negotiation and peer mediation. At the secondary level, natural peer helper programs are another format for practicing crucial life skills (Varenhorst 1992). In addition, the "creative conflict resolution" programs that Lantieri (1994) has developed are transforming hostile climates in New York City schools.

2. Early Intervention

We can identify students at risk for violence as early as the 1st grade and provide a variety of corrective experiences in the school, home, and community. We must:

   • Mentor children at risk. Millions of children suffer from affect hunger. There are not enough professional care givers for this famine, but mentoring programs offered by schools, social agencies, churches, and businesses are mobilizing a small army of adult volunteers (Freedman 1993). A unique program in Washington, D.C., schools trains at-risk adolescents to mentor elementary students (Schneider, in press). Extremely antisocial

youths who provoke rejection may respond to a team of adult
mentors who create an "attachment immersion" experience
(Brendtro and Banbury 1994).

   • Mentor and train parents. Because much early antisocial
behavior is caused by inconsistent and harsh discipline, schools
are using parent training to break coercive cycles and initiate
positive parent-child interactions.

   • Target school bullies. Peer harassment is an early indica-
tor of lifelong problems. Without intervention numerous childhood bullies become adult felons. The technology for bully-
proofing schools developed in Scandinavia is being transferred
to American schools (Hoover and Juul 1993).

   • Reach resistant students. Curwin and Mendler's "discipline with dignity" model (1988) offers teachers a system for respectful, noncoercive management of difficult students. In addition, Life Space Crisis Intervention (Wood and Long 1991)
offers counseling strategies for transforming serious student
problems into learning opportunities.

3. Reinvention of Treatment
For two decades, traditional rehabilitation has declined as public policies have reverted to punishment and removal of our
most troubled and violent students. Because these strategies
have failed, we are positioned for "growth-centered" treatment
(Palmer 1992). Whereas older rehabilitation approaches were
preoccupied with controlling deficit and deviance, new reclaiming paradigms attempt to develop strength and resilience
(Brendtro et al. 1990, Guetzloe 1994). Educators cannot solve
these problems alone. In new collaborations, mental health
workers, alcohol counselors, and justice professionals are moving into schools for front-line prevention. By investing in counselors instead of huge security forces, schools can intervene
more effectively and at less cost.

   This new psychology calls for new roles for students as well
as professionals. With adult-wary students, adult-dominated
methods backfire. Coercion feeds rebellion and fosters delinquent subcultures. The antidote to aggression and hedonism is
to get students hooked on helping. Schools that enlist antisocial
students as partners in their own healing are creating prosocial
adult and peer bonds (Vorrath and Brendtro 1985).

Because normal and dysfunctional behavior grow from the same roots, we prevent and remedy student behavior problems by meeting developmental needs. Thus the four *A*'s of the reclaiming school ethos are:

- *Attachment:* Positive social bonds are prerequisites to prosocial behavior.
- *Achievement:* Setting high expectations means refusing to accept failure.
- *Autonomy:* True discipline lies in demanding responsibility rather than obedience.
- *Altruism:* Through helping others, young people find proof of their own self-worth.

We all must make it our business to help reclaim violent students. The alternative is to discard them.

REFERENCES

Brendtro, L., and J. Banbury. (1994). "Tapping the Strengths of Oppositional Youth." *Journal of Emotional and Behavioral Problems* 3, 2: 41–45.

Brendtro, L., M. Brokenleg, and S. Van Bockem. (1990). *Reclaiming Youth at Risk: Our Hope for the Future.* Bloomington, Ind.: National Educational Service.

Brendtro, L., N. Long, and J. Johnson. (1993). "Alcohol and Kids: Facing Our Problem." *Journal of Emotional and Behavioral Problems* 2, 3: 2–4.

Charney, R. (1993). "Teaching Children Nonviolence." *Journal of Emotional and Behavioral Problems* 2, 1: 46–48.

Curwin, R., and A. Mendler. (1988). *Discipline with Dignity.* Alexandria, Va.: Association for Supervision and Curriculum Development.

Freedman, M. (1993). *The Kindness of Strangers: Adult Mentors, Urban Youth, and the New Volunteerism.* San Francisco: Jossey-Bass.

Garbarino, J. (1992). *Children in Danger: Coping with the Consequences of Community Violence.* San Francisco: Jossey-Bass.

Gold, M., and D. Osgood. (1992). *Personality and Peer Influence in Juvenile Corrections.* Westport, Conn.: Greenwood Press.

Goodlad, J. (1993). "The Occupation of Teaching in Schools." In *The Moral Dimensions of Teaching,* J. Goodlad, R. Soder, and K. Sirotnik. San Francisco: Jossey-Bass.

Guetzloe, E. (1994). "Risk, Resilience, and Protection." *Journal of Emotional and Behavioral Problems* 3, 2: 2–5.

Hoover, J., and C. Juul. (1993). "Bullying in Europe and U.S." *Journal of Emotional and Behavioral Problems* 2, 1: 25–29.

Hunt, R. (1993). "Neurobiological Patterns of Aggression." *Journal of Emotional and Behavioral Problems* 2, 1: 14–19.

Johnson, D. W., and R. Johnson. (1991). *Teaching Students to Be Peacemakers.* Edina, Minn.: Interaction Book Company.

Karen, R. (1994). *Becoming Attached.* New York: Warner Books.

Knitzer, J., Z. Steinberg, and B. Fleisch. (1990). *At the Schoolhouse Door: An Examination of Programs and Policies for Children with Behavioral and Emotional Problems.* New York: Bank Street College of Education.

Krisberg, B., and J. Austin. (1993). *Reinventing Juvenile Justice.* Newbury Park, Calif.: Sage Publications.

Lantieri, L. (1994). "Breaking Cycles of Conflict." In *Video of the National Youth Violence Summit.* Bloomington, Ind.: National Education Service.

Long, N. J. (Spring 1990). "Managing Highly Resistant Students." *Perspective:* 6–9.

Mones, P. (1993). "Parricide: A Window on Child Abuse." *Journal of Emotional and Behavioral Problems* 2, 1: 30–34.

Palmer, T. (1992). *The Re-emergence of Correctional Intervention.* Newbury Park, Calif.: Sage Publications.

Redl, F., and D. Wineman. (1957). *The Aggressive Child.* Glencoe: Free Press.

Schneider, S. (In Press). "Young Leaders Mentoring Troubled Children." *Journal of Emotional and Behavioral Problems.*

Varenhorst, B. (1992). "Developing Youth as Resources to Their Peers." *Journal of Emotional and Behavioral Problems* 1, 3: 10–13.

Vorrath, H., and L. Brendtro. (1985). *Positive Peer Culture.* Hawthorne, N.Y.: Adine du Gruyter.

Walker, H. (1993). "Antisocial Behavior in School." *Journal of Emotional and Behavioral Problems* 2, 1: 20–24.

Wood, M., and N. Long. (1991). *Life Space Intervention: Talking with Children and Youth in Crisis.* Austin, Tex.: PRO-ED.

Authors

Larry Brendtro is professor of special education at Augustana College, Sioux Falls, South Dakota, and directs the Black Hills seminars on reclaiming youth.

Kay Burke is a former teacher, an author, and a national presenter of staff development workshops. She authored *What to Do with the Kid Who . . .: Developing Cooperation, Self-Discipline, and Responsibility in the Classroom.*

Barbara C. Gartin is an associate professor in the Special Education Program, University of Arkansas, Fayetteville.

William Glasser, M.D., is a board certified psychiatrist, author, and founder and president of the Institute for Reality Therapy, Canoga Park, California. His books include *The Quality School: Managing Students Without Coercion* and *The Control Theory Manager.*

Pauline B. Gough is editor of Phi Delta Kappan.

Alfie Kohn is an independent scholar who writes and lectures widely on human behavior and education. His books include *No Contest: The Case Against Competition* and *Punished by Rewards: The Trouble with Gold Stars, Incentive Plans, A's, Praise, and Other Bribes.*

Nicholas Long is professor emeritus at American University and director of the Institute for Psychoeducational Training, Hagerstown, Maryland.

Thomas R. McDaniel is vice-president for academic affairs and provost at Converse College, Spartanburg, South Carolina. His numerous publications include the book *Improving Student Behavior.*

Nikki L. Murdick is an associate professor of special education and chair of the Department of Elementary and Special Education at Southeast Missouri State University, Cape Giradeau.

Susan J. Smith is a professor of education at Winthrop College in Rock Hill, South Carolina. She is author of *Getting a Grip on ADD* and *Getting a Life of Your Own.*

Martha Stone Wiske is a lecturer and codirector of the Educational Technology Center, Harvard Graduate School of Education, Harvard University.

Acknowledgments

Grateful acknowledgment is made to the following authors and agents for their permission to reprint copyrighted materials.

SECTION 1
Phi Delta Kappa for "The Key to Improving Schools: An Interview with William Glasser" by Pauline B. Gough. From *Phi Delta Kappan,* vol. 68, no. 4, pp. 656–662, May 1987. Copyright © 1987 by Phi Delta Kappa. Reprinted with permission. All rights reserved.

Alfie Kohn for "Caring Kids: The Role of the Schools" by Alfie Kohn. From *Phi Delta Kappan,* vol. 72, no. 7, pp. 496–506, March 1991. Copyright © 1991 by Alfie Kohn. Reprinted with permission. All rights reserved.

SECTION 2
Phi Delta Kappa and Thomas R. McDaniel for "A Primer on Classroom Discipline: Principles Old and New" by Thomas R. McDaniel. From *Phi Delta Kappan,* vol. 68, no. 1, pp. 63–67, September 1986. Copyright © 1986 by Phi Delta Kappa. Reprinted with permission. All rights reserved.

SECTION 3
William Glasser for "The Quality School Curriculum" by William Glasser. From *Phi Delta Kappan,* vol. 73, no. 9, pp. 690–694, May 1992. Copyright © 1992 by William Glasser. Reprinted with permission. All rights reserved.

The Association for Supervision and Curriculum Development (ASCD) for "How Teaching for Understanding Changes the Rules in the Classroom" by Martha Stone Wiske. From *Educational Leadership,* vol. 51, no. 5, p. 19–21, February 1994. Copyright © 1994 by ASCD. Reprinted with permission. All rights reserved.

SECTION 4
The National Association of Elementary School Principals (NAESP) for "How to Decrease Bullying in Our Schools" by Susan J. Smith. From *Principal*, vol. 72, no. 1, pp. 31–32, September 1992. Copyright © 1992 by NAESP. Reprinted with permission. All rights reserved.

Helen Dwight Reid Educational Foundation and Heldref Publications for "How to Handle Students Exhibiting Violent Behaviors" by Nikki L. Murdick and Barbara C. Gartin. From *The Clearing House*, vol. 66, no. 5, pp. 278–280, May/June 1993. Copyright © 1993 by Heldref Publications. Reprinted with permission. All rights reserved.

The Association for Supervision and Curriculum Development (ASCD), Larry Brendtro, and Nicholas Long for "Breaking the Cycle of Conflict" by Larry Brendtro and Nicholas Long. From *Educational Leadership*, vol. 52, no. 5, p. 52–56, February 1995. Copyright © 1995 by ASCD. Reprinted with permission. All rights reserved.

Index

There are
one-story intellects,
   two-story intellects, and
     three-story intellects with skylights.

All fact collectors, who have no aim beyond their
facts, are
         one-story minds.

         Two-story minds
   compare, reason, generalize,
   using the labors of the fact collectors
       as well as their own.

         Three-story minds
idealize, imagine, predict—their best illumination
comes from above,
       through the **skylight**.

—Oliver Wendell Holmes

SkyLight
PROFESSIONAL DEVELOPMENT

We Prepare Your Teachers Today for the Classrooms of Tomorrow

Learn from Our Books and from Our Authors!

Ignite Learning in Your School or District.

SkyLight's team of classroom-experienced consultants can help you foster systemic change for increased student achievement.

Professional development is a process not an event. SkyLight's experienced practitioners drive the creation of our on-site professional development programs, graduate courses, research-based publications, interactive video courses, teacher-friendly training materials, and online resources—call SkyLight Professional Development today.

SkyLight specializes in three professional development areas.

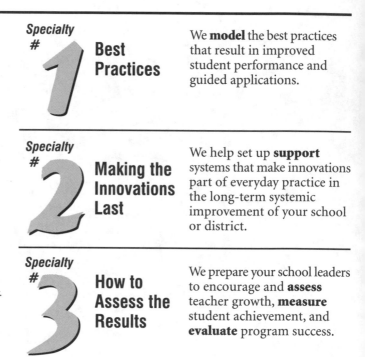

Specialty #1

Best Practices

We **model** the best practices that result in improved student performance and guided applications.

Specialty #2

Making the Innovations Last

We help set up **support** systems that make innovations part of everyday practice in the long-term systemic improvement of your school or district.

Specialty #3

How to Assess the Results

We prepare your school leaders to encourage and **assess** teacher growth, **measure** student achievement, and **evaluate** program success.

Contact the SkyLight team and begin a process toward long-term results.

2626 S. Clearbrook Dr., Arlington Heights, IL 60005
800-348-4474 • 847-290-6600 • FAX 847-290-6609
info@skylightedu.com • www.skylightedu.com